2nd Edition

Funeral Planning Basics

enodare
by enodare publishing

30682 7484

C

Bibliographic data
- International Standard Book Number (ISBN): 978-1-906144-46-3
- Edition: Second Edition (2012)
- Printed in the United States of America
- First Printing: January 2011

Published By: Enodare Limited
                        Athlone
                        Co. Westmeath
                        Ireland

Printed & Distributed By: International Publishers Marketing
                                    22841 Quicksilver Drive
                                    Dulles, VA 20166
                                    United States of America

For more information, e-mail books@enodare.com.

as affecting the validity of any trademark or service mark.

Patents

No patent liability is assumed with respect to the use of the information contained herein.

Warning and Disclaimer

Although precautions have been taken in the preparation of this book, neither the publisher nor the author assumes any responsibility for errors or omissions. No warranty of fitness is implied. The information is provided on an "as is" basis. The author and the publisher shall have neither liability nor responsibility to any person or entity with respect to any loss or damages (whether arising by negligence or otherwise) arising from the use of or reliance on the information contained in this book or from the use of the forms accompanying it.

IMPORTANT NOTE

This book is meant as a general guide to planning a funeral. While considerable effort has been made to make this book as complete and accurate as possible, laws and their interpretation are constantly changing. As such, you are advised to update this information with your own research and/or counsel and to consult with your personal legal, financial and medical advisors before acting on any information contained in this book.

The purpose of this book is to educate and entertain. It is not meant to provide legal, financial or medical advice or to create any attorney-client or advisory relationship. The authors and publisher shall have neither liability (whether in negligence or otherwise) nor responsibility to any person or entity with respect to any loss or damage caused or alleged to be caused directly or indirectly by the information or forms contained in this book or the use of that information or those forms.

ABOUT ENODARE

Enodare, the international self-help-legal publisher, was founded in 2000 by lawyers from one of the most prestigious international law firms in the World.

Our aim was simple - to provide access to quality estate planning information and products at an affordable price.

Our Will Writer software was first published in that year and, following its adaptation to cater for the legal systems of over 30 countries worldwide, quickly drew in excess of 40,000 visitors per month to our website. From this humble start, Enodare has quickly grown to become a leading international estate planning and asset protection self-help publisher with legal titles in the United States, Canada, the United Kingdom, Australia and Ireland.

Our publications provide customers with the confidence and knowledge to help them deal with everyday estate planning issues such as the preparation of a last will and testament, a living trust, a power of attorney, administering an estate, planning a funeral and much more.

By providing customers with much needed information and forms, we enable them to place themselves in a position where they can protect both themselves and their families through the use of easy to read legal documents and forward planning techniques.

The Future....

We are always seeking to expand and improve the products and services we offer. However, in order to do this, we need to hear from interested authors and to receive feedback from our customers.

If something isn't clear to you in our publications, please let us know and we'll try to make it clearer in the next edition. If you can't find the answer you want and have a suggestion for an addition to our range, we'll happily look at that too.

TABLE OF CONTENTS

AN INTRODUCTION TO FUNERAL PLANNING

Life, as we know, is transient. As such, whether we accept it or not, we have to face up to the fact that our life will come to an end at some point. Of course, we all do our best to put these types of thoughts to the back of our mind. However despite our best efforts, events will arise that give us a gentle reminder of the fact.

Often, events such as the death of a loved one or attendance at a funeral lead us to wonder about what life has in store for us in the future and what will happen to us when we die. We wonder about things such as how our family and friends will cope with our passing, what will happen to our bodies, what our funeral service will be like and so on. These types of thoughts are by no means uncommon – we're all human and we all think about these things at some stage in our lives whether we like to admit it or not.

Over the last number of years, increased attention has been given to preparing ourselves for death. The media is awash with articles on estate planning, funeral planning, end-of-life medical care, dealing with grief and so forth. Thanks to this abundance of information, preparing for death has become easier. We are generally more aware of the types of decisions we need to make, the options we have available to us and the steps we need to take to implement those options. All in all, we now find ourselves in a position where we can easily plan for our death in advance rather than simply depending on family members and friends to deal with these matters when the time arrives. This is particularly true in the context of funeral planning.

Increased consideration has been given to the subject of funeral planning over recent times and it has even become commonplace for a person to sit down with a 'consultant' and plan every aspect of their funeral service even though there is no imminent danger of that person passing away! While this may seem a little bizarre, there is a simple logic behind this tendency. Like with so many other aspects of our lives, we are becoming increasingly aware of the importance of forward planning. By planning our funeral in advance, we can reduce future costs and alleviate the unnecessary emotional difficulties that our families may endure as a result of our failure to act- whether in relation to funeral planning or otherwise.

Once spurred into getting pro-active about funeral planning, the next step will be for you to get a good understanding of what you'd like to take place following your passing. This will force you to consider a variety of different issues – many of which will be unfamiliar to you. You will have to ask yourself questions like what kind of funeral service would I want? What funeral provider should I use? Would I prefer to be interred or cremated? Am I legally required to buy items such as a casket? What ceremonial arrangements would I like to have? How much is it all going to cost and where would I get the money from?

The issue of cost is often one of the most important questions of all as your ability and desire to finance your funeral plan will have a direct impact on the options you ultimately choose for your plan. In order to get a handle on costs, it's important to speak to undertakers and funeral planners who can advise you of the likely costs involved in implementing your plans and the feasibility of your plans generally. Of course, if you want to take out an insurance policy to cover the expense of your funeral, by all means feel free to talk to your broker – otherwise the costs will be payable from your estate. You should also bear in mind that, unless you're terminally ill, you're probably going to be around for a good while yet, so any calculations which you make should take account of inflation – remember costs generally double every ten years!

Once you have done your homework and prepared your plan, it's important to keep details of your funeral plan in a safe place and of course to make both the executors appointed under your last will & testament and your close family members aware of its existence and location. When the time comes, your executors or family members can review and implement your plan. Of course, in order to ensure that your plan is properly implemented it is important that you carefully discuss each aspect of your plan with them to ensure that there are no reservations on their part in terms of implementing your plan and that they fully understand your wishes and the reasoning for same.

Having prepared a suitable plan, you can rest assured that your family isn't going to go through the added stress of trying to arrange your funeral in the manner that they believe you would have wanted, perhaps spending more than you would have approved of out of a desire to do what's best for you. Instead, when the time comes, they will have a simple plan to follow and all the necessary arrangements will have already been made to facilitate the implementation of that plan. This will make an already difficult time so much easier for them!

CHAPTER 1:
WHY FUNERAL PLANNING?

Chapter Overview

In this chapter, we will take a look at what funeral planning is and why it's so important particularly when it comes to controlling costs and ensuring that your funeral wishes are complied with.

Chapter

1

CHAPTER 1

WHY FUNERAL PLANNING?

Why Plan My Funeral?

Unfortunately, as many of us have already experienced the death of someone close to us we already know what a painful and difficult experience it is. It is a time of deep emotional turbulence for children, parents, spouses and siblings in particular. Often, they face not only the sudden shock of loosing a loved one but also a sense of fear as they contemplate the future without their loved one. It is a time when friends and family come together to support each other through a very difficult period.

In such times, the main focus is often not on the person that died but rather on the distraught relatives and friends that have been left behind. There are immediate concerns about who to notify, how to organize things and what to do generally. Whether it sounds morbid or not, issues such as organ donations, procurement of death certificates, purchasing of caskets, purchasing of grave plots, organization of funeral services, obituaries and more all have to be considered. Fortunately, through proper funeral planning you can ensure that your family and friends are not confronted with the unnecessary burden of having to consider and organize these matters on your passing. Believe it or not, a pre-arranged funeral plan will be a valued and welcome final gift to your loved ones.

Once you have decided to take the initial step of preparing your own funeral plan, it is important to remember that funeral planning is a family matter and planning should therefore start at the home. Plans should be discussed and finalized in much the same way as any other family event. While the precise funeral plan you select is largely up to you to decide upon, the support of your family for that plan will ensure that it is smoothly implemented when the time comes.

The type of funeral plan that you make is entirely up to you. Remember, there are as many ways to honor the dead as there are cultures, religions and budgets. Invariably, however, your plan will be largely influenced and guided by your faith and philosophy. All of these items will help determine whether you organize something as simple as a private cremation or whether you opt for something more elaborate like a public ceremony and a full burial service. You may even opt to have your body retained at home for private visitations by close friends and relatives, or you may decide that your body should remain at the church until burial. The options are endless and in the end come down to personal choice. Whatever options you end up choosing, be sure they are based on what's meaningful to you, not on what you think others would like or expect of you. After all, it will be part of your family's final memories of you.

Advantages of Funeral Planning

There are a number of distinct advantages to planning your own funeral. We have already touched on some of these above such as the emotional relief that it will afford to your family and of course the fact that you will get the type of funeral service that you would have wished for. However, these are not the only benefits to forward planning - there are more. We will examine some of these benefits briefly below.

(i)   <u>**Letting Your Loved Ones Know What You Want**</u>

One of the biggest mistakes that people make is adding funeral instructions in their last will only and nowhere else. This often has the unfortunate consequence that the deceased's wishes regarding their funeral service never become known until it's too late.

You should remember that when someone dies, and amongst all the emotional difficulties, the immediate focus will be on burial and taking care of the loved ones that the deceased left behind. All too often, the deceased's last will (assuming one was made) is not reviewed until after the funeral service takes place. In many cases, this is because the will is in a safe deposit box or in the deceased's lawyer's office. The result is that the deceased's wishes are often not taken into account in the planning of the funeral service.

Fortunately, by planning ahead and clearly documenting your wishes you can ensure that this type of oversight is avoided. Of course, the avoidance of this problem is very much dependent on your executors and family being made aware that you have made a funeral plan and knowing how and where to locate it when the time comes.

In reality, it doesn't take much effort to put together a basic funeral plan setting out what you would like to happen following your death.

(ii)   <u>**Relieving Your Loved Ones of Difficult Decisions**</u>

By planning ahead you will relieve your family of a huge burden and strain during an already difficult period. You can remove the necessity of having them make important decisions on your behalf. Consider, for example, the simple turmoil caused by your family being unsure as to whether you would prefer burial or cremation or even where you would prefer to be interred (if that was your preference). These are important considerations especially when your family is worried about making the wrong decision.....remember whatever decision they make is final and they will have to live with any resulting guilt, doubt or worry.

All of this can be avoided with a funeral plan. You can make all the important decisions regarding your final arrangements. You can decide whether to donate organs, whether to opt for a full traditional funeral or a simple memorial service, whether to opt for cremation rather than burial, what you want done with your ashes or where you want to have your remains interred, and so on. Making these decisions yourself will greatly help your family and, of course, by getting them involved right from the planning process you will ensure that no difficult decisions will be required in their time of difficulty.

Without the benefit of your instructions and a clear plan of action, your family will end up with additional unnecessary burdens during a difficult time – all of which could have been avoided. Believe it or not, even a simple plan outlining your preferences will go along way towards assisting your family. We have included a simple funeral arrangement plan at the back of this book to assist you prepare your plan. Feel free to use it!

(iii)   <u>Reducing the Costs of Your Funeral Service</u>

A funeral service can be quiet costly, so it certainly pays to shop around and compare and contrast the costs and services offered by the various funeral service providers in your locality. If you do not plan well in advance it is likely that you or your family will pay top prices for the service.

Often people tend to pick the funeral home closest to them or the one that their family has always used. This does not however mean that you are getting good value for money. The services provided by different funeral homes can change dramatically from one to another. If you fail to check the prices offered by other funeral homes then you may be spending well over the odds and also putting yourself under unnecessary financial strain.

Under federal regulations, funeral homes are obliged to provide you with price quotes over the phone. In addition, they are also required to present you with an itemized quotation when you show up in person to discuss funeral arrangements. As a result, you should be able to call into any funeral home and request a general or standard price list. This should enable you to readily compare the costs that different funeral service providers will charge for your funeral service. Obviously it is in your best financial interest (and your family's best interest) to compare and contrast the different prices quoted by different funeral service providers.

In addition to cost, there are other issues that you will need to consider when selecting a funeral service provider such as the staff's efficiency, helpfulness and manner. We'll discuss these aspects later in this book.

(iv)   Removing the Financial Burden of Funeral Costs

One of the major advantages associated with pre-planning is the ability to make arrangements to have the cost of your funeral discharged after your death or even paying for it in advance! Given the costs associated with funerals, removing the burden from your family of having to discharge these costs after your passing can be a blessing to them.

Generally speaking, there are three main options available when it comes to making advance preparations to pay for your funeral. The first is simply setting aside an amount of money to pay for the plan when the time comes, the second is paying for the plan in advance and the third is arranging to have insurance cover put in place to cover the cost of the plan when the time comes.

The purpose of prepaid funeral contracts is that by making all of your funeral arrangements in advance, you can ensure that your wishes are carried out and that the costs of your funeral won't impose any financial hardship on surviving family members.

By ensuring that your family has the funds necessary to pay for the plan, or by paying for it in advance, you will also make it a lot easier for them to implement the plan that you choose in the manner you choose.

Why People Fail to Plan Funerals in Advance

People's failure to plan funerals can generally be attributed to their human nature. As humans, we tend to focus on life not death and its consequences. As a result, we seldom face death as the natural part of life that it is. And, when we do face it, we tend do so with a sense of denial and an air of procrastination.

There is no doubt that many of us find it difficult to accept our own mortality and the fact that we will not live forever. As with any emotional trauma we build inner defenses to block out and ignore some of life's difficult happenings. This enables us to forgo the reality that will eventually be upon us and simply get on with things. However, while we all like to think that death is a long way off and that we can simply deal with it at some later stage, this is not always the case. No one knows when death will occur and a little forward planning can go along way in ensuring that our loved ones are not further distressed during their difficult time.

In truth, our inability to accept our mortality tends to lead to us putting off preparing for death. This couldn't be any truer than in the case of funeral planning. The mere fact of having to plan for our funeral makes the event significantly more real and, worse still, appear closer. The likelihood of having to face our own mortality head on is often enough for many to decide to 'do it another day' or even not at all. The end result for many of us is that we have no plan in place when the time comes and we simply allow the cards to fall as they may.

For many of us, therefore, the first step in preparing a funeral plan is preparing ourselves mentally. This means accepting and getting comfortable with the fact that we will eventually die. It is often only when we do this that we can bring ourselves to take the next step........making a funeral plan.

What Is Included in a Funeral Plan

Planning a funeral involves a variety of different tasks ranging from selecting a funeral planner, choosing a casket, deciding on burial and cremation options to organizing gatherings after the funeral itself. In many cases, the best people to help you with these tasks will be funeral service providers or funeral directors. They will have considerable experience in planning funeral ceremonies, preparing the deceased's body for public viewing, selecting caskets, and almost every other aspect of the funeral process. They will be able to advise you of the options available to you and ultimately help you put your plan in place.

In putting together a funeral plan you will typically need to consider matters such as:-

- whether you want to donate your body to science;

- whether you want to be buried or cremated;

- where you want your remains buried, scattered or kept;

- the type of ceremony that you will have and where it will be held;

- whether you will want visitations;

- whether you wish to be embalmed;

- whether there will be a procession to the cemetery;

- how your body will be transported;

- how your family will travel to and from services;

- the funeral products you wish to buy such as caskets, burial vaults and urns; and

- more.

But don't just visit one funeral service provider for advice and assistance. Feel free to shop around. This way, not only will you probably get a better deal but you will also get a better understanding of the different services provided by different service providers as well as the different options available to you.

We'll discuss each of the above options further in the ensuing chapters.

CHAPTER 2:
MAKING FINAL ARRANGEMENTS - FIRST STEPS

Chapter Overview

The first steps of preparing a funeral plan often include decisions about matters such as organ and body donation, transportation of your body to a funeral home and whether you want to have your body embalmed. We'll cover each of these areas in this chapter.

Chapter 2

CHAPTER 2

MAKING FINAL ARRANGEMENTS
- FIRST STEPS

Formulating a Plan

In formulating a plan for your funeral service, you need to start right at the beginning. You need to take into account everything that will happen to you from the moment you die until the time you are buried or cremated.....and even a little beyond. You will need to make choices like whether you wish to donate organs, whether you wish to leave your body on display at home or in a funeral home, what type of ceremony or funeral service you would like, whether to be buried or cremated and so on. In order to help you make these decisions, we will explore some of these various issues in the ensuing sections and chapters.

Who Should Be Notified Following Your Death

A well thought out funeral plan will usually specify who should be notified immediately following a person's death. In most cases, the first calls will be made to immediate family members as their presence is often desired to help console and comfort other grieving relatives. Family members can also be of great assistance when it comes to notifying other parties of the deceased's passing and organizing funeral services and arrangements. This is especially true when you consider the fact that family members are the people most likely to know of the existence of and location of any pre-arranged funeral plan.

Where death occurs at home, a physician will often be called in order to come and pronounce death. If death occurs in a hospital, this will usually be taken care of internally.

Calls to relatives and close friends are often closely followed by, if not preceded by, a call to the local priest or minister of faith. Having a priest or minister visit the deceased's family immediately after the death of a loved one can be of immense value to the deceased's family. Priests and ministers are often very experienced when it comes to dealing with death. They should be well positioned to provide comforting words to those who embrace their faith especially to those who embrace the concept of life after death. They will also be able to help grieving families in organizing funeral arrangements and so on.

The next person that is usually called is the funeral director. The funeral director will be able to assist with a variety of matters including the preparation of the deceased's body after death, the provision of a casket as well as the transportation of the body to a funeral home, church or cemetery. We will discuss more about the funeral director's role in the ensuing pages.

You may also want to have your lawyer, executor, work colleagues or the committee of any association that you are involved in notified of your death when the time comes. Similarly, if you have young children who need to be cared for, you may need to notify the person who will become their guardian after your passing.

In preparing your plan, you have full freedom to notify whomever you wish!

Organ Donation

One the most important issues that you should consider in preparing your funeral plan is that of organ donation. Organ donation is simply the removal of tissues and organs from the body of a person who has recently died, or from a living person, for the purpose of transplantation to another living person.

We all know of the countless people on waiting lists for organ transplantation and that the donation of organs will save lives. However, despite this many of us choose not to donate. Of course, we all have our own reasons for doing so. Some of us do it for religious reasons, some for medical reasons and some of us even do it out of fear. All of these are perfectly legitimate reasons. However, on the other hand, there are many people who would actually consider donating but never do. This is often because they are unaware of how to donate or of the precise facts about donation.

Did You Know?

According to Donate Life America:

- There are more than 100,000 men, women and children currently in need of life-saving organ transplants.

- Another person is added to the organ transplant waiting list every 10 minutes.

- On average, 18 people die daily due to the lack of available organs for transplant.

- Research shows that 98% of all adults have heard about organ donation and 86% have heard of tissue donation.

- Research shows that while 90% of Americans support donation only 30% know the required steps to becoming a donor.

- In 2009, there were 8,021 deceased organ donors and 6,610 living organ donors resulting in 28,465 organ transplants.

Resource: Donate Life America contains details on the procedures which need to be followed for organ donation in each state of the U.S. Visit their website at http:/www.donatelife.net/ CommitToDonation for further details.

Assuming that you have done your research and still wish to donate your organs for transplantation, you will be happy to know that in most cases this will be possible regardless of age or prior medical conditions. Moreover, your decision to donate will not be affected by your choice to have your remains buried or cremated.

When it comes to organ donation, you will have the choice of donating specific organs or tissue for transplantation purposes. For example, you may decide to donate your heart only and not your lungs, kidneys or eyes. In addition to being able to donate specific organs, you will also have the option of donating your entire body for medical research. There are however some limitations and restrictions on your ability to donate and these are explored in brief below.

(i)   <u>**Donation of Organs**</u>

Generally, if death takes place due to brain damage from an accident, stroke, or any event where life can be artificially sustained by machine, your body can be used to donate most major organs. This is because, in order for a person to become an organ donor, blood and oxygen must flow through the organs until the organs are extracted to ensure the viability of the transplant. However, your ability to donate would be inhibited by any medical history that displayed problems with your organs or by a serious accident which ruptured any of the organs you wish to donate. It would also be inhibited if the transplantation of organs failed to take place within a specific period of time following death. For this reason, it's important that your family and physicians are aware of your wishes in respect to organ donation so that, where possible, they can make advance arrangements for the donation of your organs when the time comes. Donated organs generally include heart, intestines, kidneys, liver, lungs and pancreas.

 Did You Know?

Donated organs and tissues can only be kept outside a living body for a short period before donation becomes impossible:

- Heart: 4-6 hours
- Liver: 12-24 hours
- Kidney: 48-72 hours
- Heart-Lung: 4-6 hours
- Lung: 4-6 hours

* Source: UNOS – United Network for Organ Sharing

(ii) **Donation of Tissues**

If you wish to donate tissues such as corneas, bone, bone marrow, skin, heart valves, veins, tendons and ligaments you can typically do this up to 24 hours after the heart has stopped beating. The removal of the cornea can often be done in the funeral home; the removal of all other tissues must take place in a surgical environment in order to properly preserve the tissue post removal. Where the cornea is removed, artificial eyes are inserted into the eye sockets and the eyes are then closed in order to facilitate the funeral service.

 Did You Know?

Tissue donated by a single person can enhance the lives of more than 50 people!

(iii) **Donation of Your Whole Body**

Many people choose to donate their bodies for scientific research or to medical departments of universities. The bodies are quite often used for teaching surgery, orthopedics, ophthalmology, cardiology, neurology, and other specialty fields. These teachings, in turn, enable the lives of many to be saved and improved. However, as with the donation of organs and tissue above, the donation of a body is subject to a number of restrictions.

Firstly, timing is again an issue. For a body to be usable, it must be collected by a medical school within a specific period of time. As such, if you die a considerable distance from the medical school, it may not be possible to have your body moved to the medical school in time.

Secondly, organ donation and body donation may be regarded as two mutually excusive programs. Generally, the donation of the whole body will not be accepted where you have donated any organs or tissue. The only real exception to this rule is in the case of the cornea of the eye which can be donated separately without resulting in a rejection of the body for full body donation purposes.

Thirdly, it will not be possible to donate the body where an autopsy has taken place or where the body has undergone the process of embalming.

Fourthly, if death occurs as a result of a disease, such as cancer or HIV, it may not be possible to donate the body.

One final point worth mentioning in the case of body donation is in respect of money. Typically, the family of the deceased never pays for the carrying out of the donation procedures. These costs, if any, are discharged by the medical school or research facility. By the same token, medical schools and state anatomical boards in the United States are prohibited by law from purchasing bodies from families. So the bottom line is that, your family should expect to neither pay money nor receive any.

After organ and tissue donation it is possible to have a normal funeral. Even with the removal of organs and tissues, the body will not appear damaged in any way and, if you wish, an open casket ceremony will still be possible. Organ donation can be completed in as little as a few hours and should not delay your funeral arrangements. If you donate your entire body to research you could consider having a memorial service (without your body present) if it will not be possible to have a funeral within the time limit set out by the research facility for collection of your remains.

The decision as to whether you wish to donate your organ or body is entirely up to you – almost! The Uniform Anatomical Gift Act, which has been adopted by almost all states, seeks to regulate the manner in which organ and tissue donations may be made. The act requires the donor to give a clear indication that he or she is willing to be an organ donor. This usually takes the form of an express statement in a will, advance directive or on an organ donor card. In addition, in order to make the process easier, many states also allow the donor to note their consent on the back of their driving license or state identity card. Surprisingly, however, notwithstanding that a person has given a clear indication of their desire to donate, the law still allows close family relatives to dissent to the procedure.

It also provides that, in the absence of any express statement by a deceased person indicating their desire to donate, the deceased's surviving spouse, or if there is no spouse, certain close relatives can give their consent to the making of an anatomical gift. However, to protect an individual against a spouse or family member deciding to donate the individual's organs against their wishes following death, the act also allows individuals to sign a refusal baring others from making any decisions in respect of the donation of their organs or tissues.

As mentioned above, the majority of states have signed up to the Uniform Anatomical Gift Act. Details of the states which have signed up to the act are set out in the diagram below.

Uniform Anatomical Gift Act - 2006

From the foregoing, you will no doubt appreciate the value of discussing your donation wishes with your family and securing their acceptance for same. In addition, if you decide to become an organ donor, you should not only fill out your wishes in your funeral plan or indeed in your will, but you should also fill out a donor card and carry it with you at all times. This will enable hospital personnel to comply with your wishes if and when the time comes.

If you wish to make a whole body donation, you will need to make prior arrangements with the medical school or research facility you have chosen to receive your gift. In many cases, a decision to donate a whole body cannot be made by the family without these prior arrangements first being in place. Again, you should expressly state in your will or advance directive or donor card what you wish to have done with your body.

It is your own personal choice whether donation is right for you. Only through careful thought and reflection can you come to a decision that is right for you. Whatever choice you make, remember to discuss it with your family and make any advance arrangements necessary.

Resource

For detailed information on all aspects of organ and tissue transplants, visit http://www.transplantliving.org or contact UNOS (United Network for Organ Sharing) patient services staff for assistance on (888) 894-6361 Monday through Friday, 8:30 am to 5:00 pm, ET.

Donating Your Body to a Body Farm

A body farm is a research facility in which human remains are deposited in a variety of different settings in order to study the decomposition of the human body in each setting. For example, bodies may be placed in a lake, forest, open hillside, desert environment or even in the boot of a car! Detailed observations and records of the decomposition process are meticulously maintained, including the sequence and speed of decomposition and the effects of insect activity on the body.

The purpose behind these studies is to help forensic anthropologists gain a clearer understanding of the decomposition process of human remains. In turn, this allows for the development of techniques which can be used to extract information from human remains such as details of the origin and identify of the body as well as details of the timing and circumstances of death.

Did You Know?

Forensic anthropology is the study and analysis of human remains for the purpose of assisting a criminal investigation. When a body is discovered, a forensic anthropologist is usually called to the crime scene to help collect and analyze the remains.

Body farms are often used as 'laboratories' where forensic anthropology students and law enforcement personnel can learn about the environment's effects on a body, while at the same time observe the body's decomposition process up close.

There are five major body farm facilities in the United States. These are situated at the University of Tennessee in Knoxville, Texas; Western Carolina University in Cullowhee, North Carolina; Texas State University in San Marcos, Texas; Sam Houston State University in Huntsville, Texas; and California University of Pennsylvania near Pittsburgh – with the Texas State University being the largest.

Each facility has a different focus for its studies. For example, the Tennessee body farm studies decomposition under a range of different conditions including buried, unburied, underwater and more. The body farm at Western Carolina focuses on decomposition in the mountainous region of North Carolina; while the body farm at Texas State University provides region-specific data on decomposition in desert like areas.

The bodies used in these research facilities are derived from a variety of different sources. While some may have lain unclaimed at the coroner's office others have been donated voluntarily to the facilities.

However, donating your body to a body farm facility will not be everyone's cup of tea. In fact, the mere thoughts of having your body laid out, decomposing in the open air (or even in a car boot!) may be enough to turn many people off the idea. On top of that, religious and personal beliefs and traditions regarding burial of the dead also deter people from the idea. On the other hand, if you are actively considering donating your body to a body farm, it's important that you have a clear understanding of what's involved.

Generally, when a body is donated to a body farm, it will be collected by the facility and placed in a refrigerator similar to those found in a morgue. It will then be assigned an identification number and placed in a specific location on the grounds of the body farm. Once placed, the location of the body will be carefully mapped so that it can be located and studied on subsequent dates. When the body farm is done with your remains, it will either cremate the remains and return them to your family or place the skeletal remains in storage at the facility. Remember to discuss this with the facility operators!

If you are interested in donating your body to a body farm then you should contact the nearest facility and make arrangements to meet with them and discuss future arrangements. You should also consider visiting the facility in question to satisfy yourself as to the precise manner in which the facility proposes to study your remains. It is also very important to discuss your choices with your immediate family so that they will honor your wishes when the time comes. Remember, they will be the ones responsible for notifying the facility of your death and ensuring that your body is actually sent to the facility. You will of course need them to respect your wishes regarding the disposal of your body otherwise there will be a risk that your wishes may not be honored.

Where proper advance arrangements are made with a body farm facility, the facility will usually arrange for the immediate collection of the donated body after funeral services have been held. Note that you cannot be embalmed for the funeral service! Normally, the facility will bear the cost of transporting the body to the facility (but will not pay your estate for the body!!!). However, if you live greater than 100 to 200 miles (depending on the facility) away from the facility, your estate may have to discharge some or all of the related transportation costs.

Important Tip

If you do not wish to have a funeral service with your body present, you could always consider having a memorial service at a later date at which your body will not be present.

Remember to explore your options carefully and make full enquiry of the facility in question before making any decision!

Resource

- University of Tennessee - Forensic Anthropology Center - http://web.utk.edu/~fac/

- Texas State University - Forensic Anthropology Center - http://www.txstate.edu/anthropology/facts/

- Western Carolina University - Forensic Research Facility - http://www.wcu.edu/293.asp

- Sam Houston University - Southeast Texas Applied Forensic Science - http://www.shsu.edu/~pin_www/T@S/2009/bodyfarm.html

- California University of Pennsylvania - Institute of Criminological & Forensic Sciences - https://www.calu.edu/business-community/forensics-institute/index.htm

Cryonics

No discussion on funeral planning or death for that matter would be complete without delving a little into the science of cryonics. Cryonics is a science that was developed in the 1960's with the view of preserving the bodies of dead people who could no longer be kept alive by conventional medicine until such time as a future technology allowed them to be healed and resuscitated.

With cryonics, immediately following a patient's death, their body is cooled to a temperature (between -150° C (-238° F) to absolute zero (-273° C or -460° F)) where physical decay ceases. This cooling is achieved through a process which involves immersing the body in liquid nitrogen. Once frozen, the body will remain stored at this temperature until such time as the technology exists to reanimate the patient and cure whatever disease he or she might have been suffering from. However, it's important to note that no clear means of reviving a person from cryostasis yet exists.

 Did You Know?

While less than 200 people have been placed in cryostasis since it was first proposed in 1962, it is estimated that several thousand people are currently on waiting lists to undergo the process. One of the most famous people to be placed in cryostasis was baseball 'Hall of Famer' Ted Williams whose head and body were famously frozen in two separate parts!

Neuropreservation

In addition to whole body preservation, it's also possible to freeze only the head or brain in a process known as 'neuropreservation'. While you might wonder why a person would want to freeze only their head, there are in fact some reasonably logical answers.

- Firstly, it's a lot cheaper than preserving an entire body.

- Secondly, many people believe that the brain is the primary component responsible for memory and personal identity and therefore the most vital part of the body to preserve.

- Thirdly, given that reanimating the body after being in cryostasis is so complex it is believed that any future technology capable of achieving that would most likely be capable of growing new tissue and even a new body around the repaired brain (and head if included). With the recent success of scientists in growing a small set of kidneys from just DNA, one can see how this belief is feasible – at least to the lay man!

- Fourthly, it is generally believed that the preservation of the brain in isolation gives it the best chances of being safely resuscitated after cryostasis. However, despite this view, academics also believe that the growth of a new body or the transplant of a new body to the brain or head following cryostasis could be fraught with complications (No surprise there!). As such, it is the preference of many cryogenic facilities to deal with whole body preservation only.

Neuropreservation will not be for everyone so be sure to do plenty of research before making a decision on it!

Financial Issues

Cryogenics, as you might well imagine, doesn't come cheap! In fact, prices range from as little as $28,000 to as high as $200,000 depending on the process required and the facility providing the service. In addition to large once off lump sum payments like this, many facilities also charge annual membership fees for the duration of a patient's 'stay'. These fees range from about $300 to $500 a year but do vary from facility to facility.

Given the large lump sum payment required and the fact that membership fees will need to be paid for many years, it is common to use life insurance to pay for the service. This allows customers to spread the cost of the process over many years through the payment of insurance premiums making it much more affordable that one might at first think – especially for younger people!

In addition to life insurance, the payments can be funded through the use of a trust or annuities.

Many facilities offer a variety of payment plans so if you are considering cryogenics as an option you should contact a number of facilities to see what payment solutions they offer.

Resources

- The Cryogenic Institute – (offers cryopreservation services and information regarding cryogenics) - http://www.cryonics.org
- The American Cryogenics Society - http://americancryonics.org
- Alcor Life Extension Foundation - http://www.alcor.org
- Suspended Animation Inc - http://www.suspendedinc.com

Funeral Service

Given that your body will need to be transported to the cryogenics facility as soon as possible following death, it will generally not be possible to have a funeral service. That said, there have been situations where bodies have been transported to facilities many hours after dying. However, it is believed that the longer it takes to place the body in cryostasis the more damage that will occur to the body and brain due to decay. In turn, this could make a successful reanimation much more difficult. As such, it makes a lot of sense to have a pre-arranged plan with the cryogenics facility in relation to how your body will ultimately be transferred to the facility in question. Most facilities will be able to advise you of the required protocol in this respect. It may even be the case that representatives of the facility could attend with you in hospital to ensure a smooth transfer of your body to the facility following death.

In addition to timing issues, matters like embalming the body and autopsies also adversely affect the cryogenics process.

If you wish to have your body placed in cryostasis, it usually makes sense to have only a memorial service without the body present - rather than any form of funeral service with the body present.

Transportation of the Body to a Funeral Home

Once your wishes (if any) regarding organ and body donation have been complied with, or refused, the next step will be to arrange for your body to be transported to the funeral home (assuming that your remains are not being transferred directly to a research facility). Here, the funeral service providers will prepare the body for public viewing and organize any funeral service that you wish to take place in the funeral home. We'll discuss more on the funeral service itself in a later chapter.

The cost of transportation will be included in the cost of the overall funeral package. Funeral services providers are obliged to give you an itemized bill setting out the precise costs of each individual service they provide for you so be sure to check the cost with them.

Preparation of the Body - Embalming

Once the body has arrived at the funeral home, the next step will be for it to be embalmed. Embalming is a surgical technique used to disinfect, preserve and restore the human body following death to an acceptable physical appearance. It involves the removal of all blood and gases from the body and the insertion of a disinfecting fluid. The majority of bodies in the United States and Canada are embalmed, though it is not required by law in most cases.

Embalming serves two main purposes. Firstly, it preserves the appearance of the body for a period of time between death and burial to allow people observe social and religious customs such as visitations, wakes, mass and funeral services. Secondly, it serves to prevent the spread of infection.

Important Note

If you are opting for a natural burial, it will generally not be possible to have your body embalmed. In that case, your body will usually be left refrigerated in order to facilitate a short viewing before burial.

In addition to embalming, cosmetic work is often carried out on the body and on the face in particular. While this is not specifically intended to make the person appear exactly like they were when they were living, it is intended to help enhance the general appearance of the deceased and allow for viewing. This is important because, quite often, when people see a deceased person it is that memory of how they look that sticks with them. The viewing of the body is very important because it allows people to come to terms with the actuality of a person's death and allows them to commence the grieving and healing processes.

While embalming is generally not required as a matter of law, it is generally carried out. As such, it will most likely feature as a cost in your funeral plan. The cost for preparation of the body including embalming, cosmetology and dressing ranges from funeral service provider to funeral service provider. Typically, the cost can vary from around $300 to $1,300 with the average cost coming in at around $750. Of course, if the funeral home provides clothing for the deceased, the cost will be at the upper end of this scale and even higher depending on the type of clothes provided.

One thing that should be pointed out is that despite any assurances you might receive from funeral service providers neither embalming nor a specific casket can prevent the decay of a body indefinitely. Nature will takes its course one way or the other so be careful about being sucked into to buying additional extras which serve little real purpose in the long run.

Once a body has been embalmed, it will be ready for public viewing. The next step will be to get ready for the viewing and any other planned ceremonies.

Did You Know?

The Federal Trade Commission introduced a set of guidelines known as 'The Funeral Rule' in 1984. The guidelines oblige funeral service providers to make certain disclosures regarding the nature of their products and services and to provide clear itemized quotations for same. The Funeral Rule statement on embalming requires funeral service providers to inform consumers that the law does not require embalming (save in a small number of special cases).

CHAPTER 3:
NOTIFYING PEOPLE ABOUT YOUR DEATH

Chapter Overview

In this chapter, we will look at some of the more common ways of notifying people of a death including traditional mediums such as newspaper and radio as well as more modern means such as the internet and social networking websites.

CHAPTER 3

NOTIFYING PEOPLE ABOUT YOUR DEATH

Notification of Death

When a person dies, it is common to notify the deceased's family, friends, colleagues and associates of the death. These notices are typically called obituaries. The main way of doing this is placing an advertisement in one or more local newspapers circulating in the area where the deceased lived and perhaps in any areas where the deceased resided for a significant length of time. Alternatively, notices may be advertised during obituary readings on local radio stations.

Obituaries

An obituary is a notice that is usually placed in a newspaper announcing that a particular person has died. It generally includes a short account of that person's life, details of the deceased's family, a note of gratitude to those who helped the deceased and the deceased's family through the bereavement, details of the proposed funeral arrangements, and a statement in respect to the provision of flowers and/or charitable donations. Where the notice omits to provide details of the deceased's life, it is generally referred to as a death notice rather than an obituary.

Obituaries and death notices are usually placed by the family of the deceased or by the funeral service provider. However, family members can sometimes find it difficult to place a notice. This is because, due to the risk of prank notices and identification mistakes, most newspapers have specific policies in relation to the publication of obituaries and death notices. In many cases, the newspapers will not publish either without sight of a copy of the death certificate or without receiving specific confirmation of the death from the funeral service provider. Generally, only immediate family members will have access to the death certificate thus limiting the family members that can place notices.

Obituaries and the Internet

While obituaries were traditionally the realm of newspapers and magazines, the advent of the internet age has brought with it a new way of publishing obituaries. Dozens of new websites have sprung up over the last few years providing free and paid locations to publish death notices and obituaries. One such website is Tributes.com (http://www.tributes.com), a site which offers several online services including obituary news information, and funeral announcements.

Even social networking sites such as Facebook, My Space and LinkedIn have got in on the act. Each of these sites has seen a substantial rise in pages created by friends and families as a memorial to a deceased loved one. And these pages are not just the realm of celebrities and crazed fans – thousands of memorial pages have been created for ordinary people with very ordinary lives. These sites offer a place where people can pay their respects to a deceased person as well as send messages to them after they have gone. They even allow you to post memorable pictures of the deceased. All in all, these types of pages have become somewhat of a virtual shrine for deceased people often with hundreds of people posting condolences and paying tributes.

As part of your obituary publications, you may also wish to have your obituary listed on one of the many online sites or even allow someone to turn your social networking site into an online shrine after you have passed away. However, just a reminder, someone will need your password and access codes to operate the account after you pass away; or alternatively, they can simply create a new account or page.

On the other hand, if you would like to have your social networking account closed, then you can leave instructions for a loved one to do so on your behalf. General contact details are listed in the resource box below.

Resources

- Facebook – deceased member notification – http://www.facebook.com/help/contact.php?show_form=deceased

- MySpace – deceased member notification – http://faq.myspace.com/app/answers/detail/a_id/369/~/delete-or-access-deceased-user's-profile

- LinkedIn – deceased member notification – http://help.linkedin.com

- Tributes.com - online tribute site - http://www.tributes.com

- Obituary Central - obituary and cemetery searches - http://www.obitcentral.com

- Obituary Links Page - obituary listing site - http://www.obitlinkspage.com

- Archives.com - historical family records - http://www.archives.com

Format of an Obituary

Obituaries generally follow a specific format. In most cases the format will be something like the following:-

- the name and address of the deceased;

- the age of the deceased at the time of death;

- the dates of birth and death of the deceased; **

- the deceased's city and state of birth;

- a synopsis of the deceased's life;

- details of any schools attended by the deceased;

- details of any employments held by the deceased;

- details of any memberships the deceased had as well as any honors they received;

- a list of survivors, starting with the deceased's spouse and children then siblings and immediate family;

- a list of immediate family members that predeceased the deceased;

- the name, address and phone number of the funeral service provider in charge of funeral arrangements;

- details of the time, date and location of the wake, visitations, funeral service and any subsequent reception;

- details of any other memorial, vigil, or graveside services to be held;

- the name of the person(s) who will be officiating at the ceremonies;

- the names of pallbearers;

- the place of interment or cremation;

- a list of where flowers may be sent or donations made in honor of the deceased;

- a note of gratitude to people, groups, or institutions;

- a favourite quotation or poem; and

- three words that sum up the deceased's life.

** Note - See section on identity theft below.

Having a Family Member Write Your Obituary

There is no hard and fast rule in terms of who should write an obituary. It usually falls to family members, close friends or the funeral service provider to write it. Of course, if you are so inclined, you can always write your own obituary!

More often than not, close family members are best placed to write obituaries as they will be familiar with the deceased's past and will be in a good position to speak to other family members and close friends in order to obtain all the information necessary to write the obituary. From their perspective, it's often a good idea to secure a copy of the deceased's resume. This should list general details about previous jobs held, achievements, honors, memberships and so on. This basic information can then be supported by other information and stories received from people who knew the deceased. The information shouldn't be too hard to get as people are often very fond of recanting tales of the deceased's exploits following their death and may therefore be happy to add their little trinket of information.

Sample of a Simple Obituary

John Furlong, 77

John Furlong, 77, of New York City, died January 10, 2011, at his home in Queens.

Mr. Furlong was born in August 1933, in Houston, Texas, to Ambrose and Amanda (nee McHenry) Furlong.

He attended Milby High School in Houston. He continued his education at Harvard University in Cambridge, Massachusetts, graduating in 1954 with an associate's degree in business studies.

A keen fan of the New Jersey Nets, he enjoyed playing basketball and sailing; as well as attending Broadway shows with his family.

He is survived by his brother Thomas Furlong; and his partner Eva Gibson of Manhattan.

He was preceded in death by his parents Ambrose and Amanda.

Arrangements are with Manhattan Central Funeral Home.

Write Your Own Obituary

While it may not happen too frequently, it's not unheard of that a person would write their own obituary. That said, for many it's simply too morbid a task to broach. However, if you are thinking of writing your own obituary it is certainly to be encouraged as it offers you a personalized way of saying goodbye to your friends and recalling the significant aspects of your life in a way that you would like.

A good place to start when writing an obituary is to contact the newspaper(s) that you intend publishing the obituary in and see what requirements they might have in terms of word limitations, format, etc. You should also check out the price while you are at it.

Once you know the parameters that you are required to write within, the next step is to get researching. You should carefully review the items listed above in the "Format of an Obituary" section as well as the checklist provided in connection with the writing of an obituary (see next page). You should then jot down as much information as you can in relation to each of the headings/topics that you wish to write about. The information does not have to be 100% complete – it just needs to be sufficient to give you an indication of the content which you will be including in the obituary. Once you have this done, you should review a number of obituaries online. A simple search of the term "sample obituaries" on Google will bring up hundreds of results. You should read through a few obituaries noting the style and composition of each. These should give you an overall understanding of the format and direction you want to take with your own obituary.

Once you have carried out the above tasks, the next step is to write the obituary itself. Again, there are multiple websites which will give you further guidance on how to do this. However, in most cases, the sample format set out above and the sample obituaries you viewed online will be sufficient. Once your first draft is complete, you will need to review and edit it several times before settling on a final version. This can be a cumbersome process but will certainly be worth it in the end. And remember to check your spellings! Incorrect spellings are the number one problem associated with obituaries.

Tips for Writing an Obituary

- Check spellings.

- Make sure the names of people, places and organizations are spelled correctly.

- Make sure that facts and details are accurate – while it may be nice to brag sometimes...an obituary is certainly not the place to do it!

- Make the obituary lively and positive - refrain from focusing on negative points about your life.

- Identify characteristics about yourself using stories rather than simply listing them. For example, show that you were charitable by giving actual examples, rather than just saying you were "charitable."

- Describe the deceased as an individual, in the third person.

- Revise and edit. As with any writing, revising improves the final product by allowing you to spot mistakes and improve the style and flow of the writing

- Proofread the final product – then proofread it again!

Costs

As you will probably guess, the cost of placing an obituary in a newspaper varies from paper to paper. In some cases, the newspaper will publish a standard obituary for free in its obituary section. In other cases, the newspaper will charge a fee for including the obituary as well as any photos that you want to accompany it. You will need to ring the newspapers in which you wish to publish the obituary to confirm their fees.

Identity Theft and Simple Theft

Before closing off on the subject of obituaries, it's important to briefly mention the concept of identification theft which, thanks mainly to the internet, has become a serious problem in recent years.

Identity theft occurs where unscrupulous people obtain personal details about someone (living or dead) and use those details for the purpose of committing a fraud or some other crime. In recent times, the concern of identity theft has caused many people to withhold specific personal details from obituaries – especially details such as the deceased's date of birth. In writing an obituary, you will need to find a balance between the information that you need to include to allow people identify the deceased and that which ought to be protected to prevent identity theft. Very often it helps to cut off the deceased's credit cards, back cards and bank accounts immediately following the deceased's death. This will certainly make it more difficult to steal the deceased's identity.

The other thing that you need to be careful about is providing the specific home address of the deceased. In many instances this will be taken as a notice to potential thieves that the house will be unattended during the hours of the funeral service! Be cautious!

Conclusion

Writing an obituary isn't that difficult if you stick to the standard guidelines set out above and review a number of online obituaries. Even the most inexperienced of writers should be able to prepare a relatively straight forward obituary with little help. However, if you feel you need assistance, by all means ask a friend to assist or even the funeral director. The latter will be particularly well experienced in writing obituaries and should be happy to assist you. It may even be a good idea to have the funeral director review the obituary before you submit it to the paper – just in case!

Resources

- Obituary Guide.com – tips and help on writing an obituary - www. obituaryguide.com

- Obituaries Help.org – help, tips and sample obituaries www. obituarieshelp.org/sample_obituaries_hub.html

- Elegant Memorials – sample obituaries – www.elegantmemorials.com/ how-to-write-an-obituary/sample-obituaries

- Funeral Program Site – sample obituaries and sample template - www. funeralprogram-site.com/funeral-planning/sample-funeral-obituary

- Caring.com – obituary template and real obituaries - www.caring.com/ obituary-sample

CHAPTER 4:
PREPARING FOR THE FUNERAL SERVICE

Chapter Overview

The funeral service will be your last goodbye. As such, You should give a lot of thought as to what you want as your final send off. You will need to consider things like visitation, ceremonies, desired music and readings, and much more. We'll explore your options in this chapter.

Chapter 4

CHAPTER 4

PREPARING FOR THE FUNERAL SERVICE

Decide On the Type of Ceremony

Your final ceremony will be a lasting memory in the minds of many of your friends and relatives. It is therefore important to give it due care and attention. You will need to consider whether you would like to go with a traditional funeral service synonymous with your religious beliefs or go with a more modern approach like a memorial to your life. Of course, you may also choose to have neither and go with something completly different. The choice is entirely up to you. However, assuming you decide to hold some type of ceremony, you will need to carefully organize and plan for it in advance.

Funeral directors can be of great assistance in helping you plan ceremonies in advance and can subsequently help direct the ceremonies in accordance with your wishes when the time comes. They will often have the staff, facilities, and equipment necessary to fulfill your ceremonial wishes. They will also have good contact with local cemeteries, churches, venues, music groups, and florists amongst others. So do not make the mistake of underestimating their potential value when it comes to preparation. Of course, your family members and close friends will also play a major role when the time comes. It is therefore important to discuss your choices and preferences with each group once you have decided on what you want. That way, you can address any questions or concerns that they might have and help ensure matters run smoothly when the time comes.

Funeral Service

A funeral service is a formal service based on the religious or cultural beliefs of the deceased. It typically involves a member of the clergy conducting a ceremony at either the home of the deceased or in a funeral home. Friends and family of the deceased will normally attend and will pay their last respects to the deceased as well as their condolences to the immediate family of the deceased. The deceased's remains are then usually transported to the church where the ceremony is continued with hymns, scripture readings, a short sermon, and sometimes a eulogy. After that, the deceased's remains are removed by procession to the cemetery for burial or crematorium for cremation. In the case of burial, a brief graveside service is usually conducted. Once the burial or cremation has taken place, it is customary for friends, relatives and other mourners to gather at the family home or a pre-selected venue for further expressions of sympathy.

One of the primary differences between funeral services and memorials is that with the former the body of the deceased is usually present during the service. As the body is normally present during the service itself, the service typically takes place within a few days of the deceased's death.

If you opt for a traditional funeral service, there are a number of matters that you will need to give thought and attention to. These include:

- the initial ceremony at the family home or in the funeral home;

- clothing and styling;

- the funeral mass;

- readings;

- flowers;

- music;

- transportation;

- pall bearers; and

- grave side ceremony.

We'll discuss each of these matters briefly below.

The Initial Ceremony

The initial ceremony basically consists of the laying out of the deceased's body so that people can come and say their final goodbyes to the deceased as well as pay their condolences to the deceased's family.

The first thing that you will need to decide about regarding the ceremony is whether to hold it in your family home or in the funeral home. This will be a matter of individual choice. From a cost perspective, the latter option will of course be more expensive. That said, the holding of the ceremony will not be without some cost irrespective of the venue. Don't forget, it's likely that friends and relatives will be visiting and refreshments will need to be organized, purchased and served.

The other thing you will need to consider is whether you would like to have an open casket. An open casket is simply a casket that remains open to allow people see the remains of the deceased. Many experts believe that an open casket is very important for surviving relatives and friends as the sight of a deceased loved one is often the first step in accepting that the deceased has passed away and in commencing the grieving process. However, the choice as to whether you have an open or closed casket is entirely up to you. That said, there are circumstances in which the casket may be closed notwithstanding your wishes. This generally occurs where the condition of the body has been adversely affected by an accident or injury.

Whatever your choices are, it's important to discuss them with both your family and funeral director as they will be the people responsible for organizing the venue and service when the time comes. They will also be able to organize things like flowers, candles and so on. There may even be a favorite room in the house where you would like to be placed or some music you would like to have playing in the background. So be sure to tell them what you want in as much detail as possible and be sure to put it down in your funeral plan.

Clothing and Styling

One thing that is often overlooked by many people in preparing funeral plans is the clothing that they wish to be dressed in for their funeral service and burial. Many people have a favorite suit or dress or even a military uniform that they would like to be dressed in. As well as that, people often forget to mention that they want to have their hair styled in a particular fashion, to have makeup put on or even to wear specific jewelry or decoration (such as medals). So, remember to specify your wishes as precisely and conclusively as possible in your funeral plan.

If you would prefer something new to be purchased for your funeral, be sure to state that. Remember to factor in the costs of any new clothes when considering the overall costs of your funeral plan.

Funeral Mass

Your funeral mass should be a special memory for your family and loved ones. However, unless it is planned in advance, your family and loved ones may have to arrange it in a hurry. If this happens, there is a risk that it may be less meaningful than it could have been. Fortunately, with a little planning you can ensure that the service is conducted in the way that you would like and is both special and memorable to your loved ones. The good news is that you don't have to do anything extravagant. You just have to give it some careful consideration.

Planning a funeral mass is relatively straight forward, all you generally need to do is make some choices about hymns, prayers, readings and flowers for the mass.

You can also decide on the gifts that you would like to be brought to the altar, whether communion is to take place and whether a family member or friend reads a tribute or eulogy about you.

Of course, each religion is different and each has its own ritual and beliefs. You will of course have to design your own ceremony and funeral plan around these beliefs. In the ensuing sections, we will briefly examine some of the most popular areas of the funeral service which people like to customize.

Participants in the Ceremony

The first thing that you will need to consider is who will take charge of and officiate at the ceremony. Usually, this task is handled by a member of the clergy or a trusted friend. You will then need to consider what other people you want to have involved in the ceremony. Maybe you have a son or daughter that you would like to do a reading or a favorite niece who you would like to sing a song at the ceremony.

If there is someone in particular that you would like to deliver a memorial speech or eulogy on your behalf you may need to let them know in advance and not simply rely on having it noted in your funeral plan.

Other participants could be singers, poetry readers or candle lighters.

Readings

If you would like to have someone read from the scriptures or from a favorite book or poem, you will need to ensure that you nominate them in your funeral plan and, more importantly, make some arrangement to have the pieces available when the time comes. You could even consider attaching them to the back of your funeral plan.

Flowers

Flowers have both an aesthetic effect and a calming effect and bring warmth to a room. They may even bring some comfort to mourners. If you have any

favorite flowers that you would like to include at your funeral, again specify it in your plan. If you want them arranged in a certain manner this should also be specified.

Decorations

Apart from flowers, there are numerous other decorations that you may wish to have at your funeral ceremony. These may include:-

- plants;

- candles;

- displays;

- photographs;

- military decorations - flags, photos and medals;

- symbols of your life;

- and many more.

In addition to enhancing the immediate location, the decorations can act as a powerful reminder of the good times in your life. Changing the focus of mourners from the sadness of your death to fond memories of you can have a positive effect on how they cope with your loss and how they remember you. Again, if you have any wishes, note them in your plan.

Music

Music will help set the mood and atmosphere of the service. You can arrange to have your favorite musical pieces played or sung as reminders of you. If you wish to have any pieces performed at the ceremony, you will need to decide on whether:

- the piece will be sang or played with an instrument;

- a particular instrument will be used;

- a particular person or group will perform the piece;

- the piece will be played using a stereo or similar device;

- the participants sing along; and

- so on.

Transportation

You should also consider how you would like to have your remains transferred between your home, the funeral home, the church and the cemetery or crematorium. In most cases, a black hearse is used. However, people often have their own special requests when it comes to transportation. For example, some people choose to use horse drawn carriages or something which closely represents their interests in life.

You should also consider how your family will be transported between the aforementioned locations. Will they be left to make their own way or will you ask the funeral service provider to make their personal cars available.

Pall Bearers

Pall bearers are the people who traditionally carry the casket to and from the church and grave site. In most cases, they will be close relations and friends of the deceased. Usually six or more people will act as pall bearers at a funeral. If there are any people that you want or even do not want involved in this process, be sure to specify it in your funeral plan.

Graveside Ceremony

The graveside ceremony typically involves a clergy member giving a short sermon at the grave, after which the casket is usually interred. The funeral director and clergy man will usually organize all of the matters associated with this short service including the provision of chairs and audio equipment. However, if there is anything out of the norm that you want added you will need to specify this in your plan. These requests may include specific music, readings etc taking place at the graveside.

Food and Beverages

After the graveside service, it is common for many people to return to the house of the deceased person's relatives (or selected venue) to support them through this difficult period. It is common to serve light refreshments at these services as many people will have travelled long distances to attend the ceremony while others may have had little to eat during the long drawn out process since the deceased's death.

You should therefore give some consideration to whether you want to organize such refreshments and where and what should be organized.

Memorial Service

A memorial service is held without the body, so it can be scheduled days, weeks, or even months after your death occurs. This will give time for family, friends and loved ones to gather together and more importantly to get over the impact of your death.

Memorials are increasing in popularity in tandem with the increase in cremations. Although, many people have funerals and end up being cremated. If you have opted for cremation, you should also give some thought as to whether you would like to have your urn present at the ceremony.

A memorial service can be as elaborate or simple as you choose, and may be held anywhere -- at home, in a park, by the lake, at the graveside, in a church or temple, or at a funeral home or mortuary. In many ways, it is very like the funeral service described above. It acts as an event to celebrate your life and is usually attended by both family and friends. In the same way that you considered music, readings and so on for the funeral service, you can also consider the same items for the memorial service. You should also consider appointing someone to act as the master of ceremonies at your memorial.

From a cost perspective, if you plan the memorial service yourself, without the help of a funeral home director, you can expect to pay only a fee for the use of the venue. However, you should also consider extras such as food and drink, music, provision of chairs and other furniture, flowers and any other items which may be required for the memorial you have in mind.

Committal Service

In addition to funeral services and memorial services, or indeed instead of them, it's also possible to have a committal service (sometimes called a graveside service or graveside ceremony). A committal service is a brief ceremony held at the graveside following a funeral. It is usually attended by family and friends of the deceased who gather together as the casket is lowered into the grave. Flowers are often thrown in on top of the casket before a family member or grave yard worker begins to fill in the grave with soil.

Funeral directors or members of the clergy can help you organise the ceremony for the most part. However, if you want anything more elaborate than some sound equipment and chairs you may need to make your own provisions in advance or at least leave your family with details of how they might organise these items when the time comes.

It's worth remembering that committal services can also take place before cremations in much the same way as at gravesides except that they take place in the crematorium. Of course, if the ashes are to be buried post cremation, then a committal service can be held at the graveside before burial.

The costs of the committal service really depends on what you want. In most cases, your funeral service provider will be able to give you a reasonable estimate of the costs involved. The costs usually consist of transportation to the committal service site, opening and closing of the grave, provision of equipment and the provision of staff. Be sure to get full details of all costs included and include them in your overall calculations.

Ceremony Costs

Once you have decided the type or types of ceremony you want and what you want included, you will then need to give some thought to the costs of putting it all into effect. You can shop around and get quotes from individual funeral service providers and even third party providers. However, you should remember that over time these costs will increase with inflation. If you are availing of any pre-paid option, make sure that you have some form of written agreement containing a clear and accurate description of what will be provided and when. Again, any agreements that you have in this respect should be included in or attached to your funeral plan.

Memorials

A memorial can generally be described as a physical, online or written tribute to someone who has died. Traditional memorials have included items like the headstones and plaques commonly found in cemeteries; the benches found in parks, community areas and private gardens; and even sculptures. More recently, virtual memorials have started to spring up on various internet sites. All of these memorials, irrespective of type, represent a 'lasting' symbol of remembrance and a tribute to someone who has died.

Memorials come in a variety of different shapes and sizes which are usually dictated by the requirements of the places in which the memorial is to be placed. We have explored some of the common memorials below.

Memorials Located at Burial Sites

Throughout recent history, it has been common place to erect headstones or memorial markers at the site where a person has been interred. In traditional cemeteries, these markers generally consist of plaques, headstones and above-ground burial vaults. In all cases, the types and size of memorial which can be erected in the cemetery will depend on the rules and regulations of the cemetery. For more information on erecting markers at graveyards see the section on 'Headstones and Markers' in Chapter 5.

When it comes to green burials or burials in eco forests, there are severe restrictions on the types of memorials that can be placed at a burial site. While, in some cases, it may be possible to have a flat stone marker placed at the grave site or even have a marker placed on a tree, many green burial sites restrict the placing of markers outright. Where this happens, they often allow organic memorials such as trees or shrubs to be planted at the gravesite instead. Given the restrictions relating to the placing of memorials in such sites, it's important that you check the rules and regulations of the burial site carefully before purchasing or making arrangements in connection with the erection of any form of memorial.

At columbaria (plural of columbarium) and mausoleums, it is generally possible to place a small plaque on the outside of the niche or burial chamber. However, strict rules generally apply to the size and type of the plaque that can be placed.

You will therefore need to check these rules to see what options are open to you.

Memorials Located Away From Burial Sites

Where it's not possible to place a marker at a burial site, many people decide on creating some other form or memorial to mark the life of the deceased. These memorials tend to be in both public and private places. In fact, just visit your local public park or church and you're bound to find some benches that have been erected in memory of a deceased person. And, while you are wandering around that park you might even notice that trees, flower gardens and shrubs have also been planted in memory of deceased people. You may even notice statutes, bridges or lights that have been erected or labelled as memorials!

In reality, the opportunity to create lasting memorials is endless. You could even create a memorial cup for a particular sport that you were interested in or pay for the redevelopment of a library or pier and have it named after you. The choice is yours!

The costs of these memorials will vary greatly depending on what you want to erect. As such, you should carefully plan any memorial that you are intent on having and thoroughly investigate the rules relating to the erection of the memorial you want and all related costs.

Resources

- Perfect Memorials – large variety of memorials including outdoor memorials - www.perfectmemorials.com

- Memorials.com – extensive selection of memorial items - www.memorials.com

- Brick Pavers – brick and tile engraving service - www.brickmarkers.com

- American Forests - plant a tree in someone's memory for a nominal cost - www.americanforests.org/planttrees/

- Arbor Day Foundation - information on planting memorial trees - www.arborday.org/

- Memorial Matters – online memorial site - www.memorialmatters.com/

Virtual Memorials

As already mentioned, online memorials are becoming more and more popular with new sites popping up on the internet almost on a weekly basis. These sites, or at least the better sites, provide an easy and inexpensive way of creating a memorial. In fact, many of these sites actually provide a free service. For more information on these sites, see the section entitled "Obituaries and the Internet" in Chapter 3.

Choosing a Memorial

The most important thing to remember when deciding on a memorial is that you will generally have time to think about what you want. The same applies to your family if they are making the decision for you after you have passed away. There is no time limit within which the memorial must be erected. So, take the time to do your research and do it right. The internet is an excellent way to source information and prices for your memorial – so do use it!

A Final Thought On Memorials

When it comes to memorials, it really doesn't matter what type of memorial is created so long as it provides a special means by which surviving family and friends of the deceased can remember their loved one. Of course, it will always be more significant if the memorial bears some significance to the life of the deceased – such as naming part of a pier after a deceased fisherman. Take your time and think through what you want carefully. And, remember - the goal is to keep the memory of the deceased alive. How you do that is not really as relevant.

CHAPTER 5:
FINAL DISPOSITION

Chapter Overview

In planning your funeral, you will need to decide on whether you want to be buried or cremated. There are a number of matters that you will need to consider before making this decision. We'll guide you through each of these matters in this chapter.

Chapter 5

CHAPTER 5

FINAL DISPOSITION

Burial or Cremation – Advantages and Disadvantages

When it comes to the disposition of your remains, the two most popular choices open to you are burial and cremation. There are a number of advantages and disadvantages associated with each and you will need to consider these as well as your personal views and beliefs in order to decide what is best for you.

The advantages and disadvantages associated with burial include the following:

Advantages:

- It is a religious tradition and many faiths believe in the returning of the body to the earth.

- It is a family tradition and it is not uncommon for members of the same family to be buried in the same plot or in the same vault.

- Friends and family have a focal point to return to and remember you.

- It allows for the building of a permanent memorial to your life.

Disadvantages:

- The costs of burials can be expensive. This is particularly so when you add the cost of funeral services, caskets, plots, liners and so on.

- Burial can adversely affect the environment due to the large amount of metal, concrete and embalming fluids that are placed into the earth.

The advantages and disadvantages associated with cremation include the following:-

Advantages:

- It is usually much cheaper than burial.

- Saves land and can be environmentally friendly, unlike the use of metal burial vaults and caskets for example.

- The remains can be scattered or buried at a later date.

Disadvantages:

- It tends to leave the deceased's loved ones with fewer ways to morn and no focal point to remember the deceased.

- Family members may not agree on exactly what should happen to the deceased's remains after cremation. Should they be scattered at a particular site? Should they be divided amongst family members? Should they be buried?

- Not all religions approve of cremation.

In order to help you decide between burial and cremation, we will examine each of these choices in much more detail below.

Burial

Burial is the most common way of disposing of a person's remains following their death. It is a tradition incorporated into the religious beliefs of many of the World's population. At its simplest, it involves the placing of a person's remains into the ground. At its most elaborate it involves huge processions and ceremonies.

The traditional burial service is generally considered to be the most expensive type of funeral, although funerals can range in nature from basic to extravagant, depending on your personal choices. In many funeral homes the basic service incorporates embalming, dressing the body, rental of the funeral home for the viewing or service and use of the funeral service provider's vehicles to transport the family during the funeral procession. The costs of a casket, cemetery plot, marker, crypt and other funeral goods and services must also be taken in to account when calculating the cost of burial.

A traditional funeral service including burial is likely to involve many of the following aspects:

- casket;

- transfer of the deceased to the funeral home;

- embalming;

- dressing, cosmetology and other care of the deceased;

- professional support and administrative staff assistance;

- use of visitation rooms;

- general use of the facilities for the funeral service and arrangements;

- limousine;

- utility car;

- register book;

- acknowledgment cards;

- memorial folders or prayer cards; and

- so on.

These all add to the overall cost of burial. However, of all of these items, caskets remain the most expensive. The cost of caskets is covered in detail below.

Choosing a Casket

Unfortunately, choosing a casket is unlikely to be a very pleasant experience as it may well give you a renewed sense of your own mortality. Nevertheless, it should be treated in the same manner as you would approach any other significant purchase. You will need to evaluate the casket based on items like its costs, materials and design. We'll look at some of these issues below.

Picture provided courtesy of memorials.com

Cost of Caskets

A casket is generally the most expensive item that you can include in your funeral plan. While you will have a degree of control over the amount you spend on a casket, you will find that casket prices can range widely depending on the materials used and the level of internal and external design applied to the casket. Prices can range from less than $1,000 for a simple pine or pressed wood box to $15,000 or more for elaborate copper or bronze caskets with innerspring mattresses and plush velvet or silk linings.

The price of caskets is determined based on a number of factors including the:-

- type of material used to construct the casket itself. Generally, caskets are constructed of metal, wood, fiberboard, fiberglass or plastic;

- interior fabrics used in the caskets. Typical fabrics include satin, velvet, silk, crepe, gold lace and white lace; and

- detail of the overall design (types of handles used and the design on the casket itself).

On average, caskets tend to cost somewhere in the region of between $2,000 to $5,000. However, you will be able to discuss your needs with the funeral director and he or she should be able to help you find something that meets both your requirements and your budget.

It's important to be aware that funeral service providers add a premium to the price that they charge for caskets and usually sell them as part of a package. It is possible to reduce the costs of the casket by buying directly from the manufacturer or from retailers. In fact, even Wall Mart (yes Wall Mart!!) now sells caskets. Moreover, under the Funeral Rule, funeral service providers cannot charge a handling fee if you purchase a casket from a third party for your funeral.

Historic studies have shown that visitors to funeral homes or showrooms tend to purchase one of the first three caskets that they are presented with. This may well be because most funeral directors are likely to show their most popular caskets to potential customers first. However, to protect customers, the Federal Trade Commission has incorporated some sales requirements into the Funeral

Rule code that we mentioned above. Specifically, funeral directors are required to provide you with full details of all caskets that they are selling (including details of the price) before they actually show you the caskets. In this way, you will have a general appreciation for the price ranges and features of caskets before you are presented with the caskets themselves. This (it is expected) should reduce the likelihood of spending excessively on a casket simply because you were unaware of your full spectrum of options.

Once you have been presented with details of the caskets, you will most likely be brought to a showroom where you will be shown some of the more popular caskets as well as some caskets from the upper and lower price ranges. The funeral director should be able to advise you of the individual features of each casket and present you with options for added extras such as interior linings and handles.

Traditional Caskets

In the majority of cases, traditional caskets are constructed of either wood or metal.

Wooden caskets are generally constructed from hardwoods such as oak, mahogany, cherry, poplar or walnut or from softwoods like pine. Once constructed, the overall appearance of the casket is complemented by adding interior linings. The exterior of the casket will usually contain a design of some type (usually floral) and handles.

Hardwood caskets are made from a number of different woods. The main woods include:

- Mahogany: Mahogany is a generally straight grain wood and is usually free of voids and pockets. It has a reddish brown color which darkens over time, and displays a strong sheen when polished. It has excellent workability, and is very durable. Mahogany is resistant to termites and rot.

- Cherry: Cherry is a tight grain wood which ranges in color from a deep, rich red to reddish brown. It also darkens with both age and exposure to sun light.

- Maple: Maple is a strong, close grained wood that is predominantly off-white in color; although it also contains light hues of yellow-brown and pink. Hard maple occasionally contains light tan or small dark mineral streaks.

- Oak: Oak is hard, durable and highly resistant to water and other liquids. It is a strong open grained wood with a coarse texture and a straight grain. It can range in color from red to brown and can be streaked with other colors.

- Ash: Ash is a strong, straight grained heavy wood which ranges in color from off-white (sapwood) to light brown to pale yellow streaked with brown.

- Poplar: Poplar is an even-textured straight grained wood which varies in color from creamy white in the sapwood to pale yellow-brown or olive green for the heartwood. The heartwood darkens when exposed to natural light, eventually turning to a rich shade of brown. Poplar is very popular because it can be stained to look like most other types of wood.

- Wood Veneer: This is often used for lower-cost casket alternatives. A veneer is simply a thin layer of wood created in a standard thickness.

- Pine: Pine is a straight-grained durable wood with a fine texture and low contrast, often white, yellow or reddish brown in color.

- Walnut: Walnut is a strong wood with a medium to coarse texture that varies in color from white to dark brown. It is generally straight-grained but can also have wavy or curly like grain that produces an attractive and decorative figure.

As most wooden caskets are generally closed with a latch or screw like fitting, they do not offer the best protection and are not sealed against decomposition. Metal caskets, on the other hand, do offer such protection.

There are many different types of metal caskets available, each with its own unique features and advantages. The most common types include bronze, copper and stainless steal. Bronze and copper are categorized based on the weight per square foot (example - 30 ounce bronze) while stainless steel caskets are categorized based on the thickness of the steel used such as 20 gauge steel. You should note that the lower the gauge the thicker the metal.

As the metal caskets are welded together, they offer better protective qualities than traditional wooden caskets. As a result of the manner in which they are rubber sealed when closed for the last time, they are often described as 'gasketed', 'sealer' or 'protective' caskets. They are designed to delay the penetration of water into the casket and prevent rust. This delays the decomposition of the body. However, as already mentioned, they do not preserve the remains of the body indefinitely.

Resources

- Memorials.com – large range of wooden and metal caskets - www. memorials.com

- Caskets Online – operated by a Dallas based family business - www. casket-online.com

- Best Price Caskets – large range of caskets & funeral products - www. bestpricecaskets.com

- The Casket Place.com – large selection of caskets - www.thecasketplace. com

- Casket Express – low price caskets including art caskets - http:// casketxpress.com

Orthodox Caskets

Judaism, like many religions, has traditional rituals and ceremonies that take place following the death of one of its followers. Rather uniquely, however, Jewish law actually dictates certain requirements for its follower's caskets. These requirements provide that:

- simple and plain caskets should be used;

- wooden dowels should be used instead of nails or screws;

- only vegetable-based glue can be used;

- the casket must be made exclusively from wood and should have several holes drilled through its base. This allows for the speedy decomposition of the remains which facilitates the Jewish requirement to have the body returned to earth without undue delay;

- manufacture of the casket cannot occur on Sabbath; and

- the entire casket must be biodegradable. As such, only natural materials such as 'wood wool' is used for the interior of the casket. 'Wood wool' is essentially thin wood shavings.

Resources

For orthodox caskets, visit the green casket company's website at www. green-casket.com. Companies like memorials.com also sell Jewish caskets for prices starting at $1,297.95. Visit www.memorials.com.

Green Caskets

There is now a considerable selection of eco-friendly caskets on sale in the market. A quick search for green caskets or green coffins on the internet will turn up hundreds of results – reflecting the increasing environmental consciousness relating to burial. The idea behind the creation of a green casket is typically to create a casket that is easily broken down without harm to the earth. To this end, biodegradable materials such as wood and wood shavings are almost exclusively used in the manufacture of green coffins.

Companies like the Green Casket Company (www.green-casket.com) are now creating green caskets made from materials extracted from sustainable forests. The company also highlights that neither metal nor toxins (such as glues) are used in the manufacture of their caskets; while organic cotton is used for the internal lining of the casket and the enclosed pillow is filled with pine-shavings.

Similarly, Albuquerque-based Passages International (www.earthurn.com) has developed a casket made of willow, bamboo and sea grass that looks like a wicker basket.

One of the more interesting developments has come from ARKA Ecopod Limited. They have developed a revolutionary eco-friendly casket known as an "ecopod". The ecopod is hand made from recycled newspapers and finished with paper made from 100% mulberry pulp.

Green caskets are generally suitable for cremation, or burial in woodland sites or traditional cemeteries, and biodegrades naturally over time when placed in the ground. Although, if you are planning on being buried in a traditional cemetery remember that you will most likely need to purchase a burial vault.

Green coffins can also be ideal for orthodox Jewish burials.

Resources

- Ecopod - environmentally friendly caskets and urns - www.ecopod. co.uk

- Ark Wood Caskets – offers DIY pine caskets from $499 – See www. arkwoodcaskets.com

- Memorials.com – offers green caskets from only $197

Personalized Caskets

A number of casket manufacturers have sprung up over the last few years making personalized caskets or on-demand caskets. There seems to be no end to the types of caskets being made. Companies such as UK based Crazy Coffins (www.crazycoffins.co.uk) make caskets in the shape of guitars, cars, truck, footballs, football boots, mobile phones and more. There are numerous other wacky coffin makers out there and we've provided details of some of their websites in the resource box below. Just remember, if you are choosing a "crazy" coffin, be sure that the dimensions and specifications of the coffin will be acceptable to your chosen cemetery or crematorium. Don't forget, a bigger coffin means a bigger grave site and a bigger burial vault and even higher transportation fees! By the way, don't be surprised if these coffins don't come too cheap either!

Resources

- Coffin it up – want a spooky coffin for burial…seriously… - www.coffinitup.com

- Bert & Budd's Vintage Coffins – vintage gothic styled coffins - www.vintagecoffins.com

- My Funky Funeral – for some more strange funeral ideas – www.myfunkyfuneral.com

- Dying Art – New Zealand based coffin art company - www.dyingart.co.nz

Cemeteries

A cemetery is the place where the dead are buried or interred. It is, in essence, the final resting place for the dead. Cemeteries offer a variety of different types of grave plots or spaces for burial and the construction of mausoleum crypts for entombment; as well as space for the construction of markers beside graves. They also offer similar options for the burial or entombment of cremated remains.

Important Note

A grave is a single burial space whereas a plot is an area that contains more than one grave. Families often purchase plots.

If you wish to be buried you will need to consider purchasing a cemetery space. On average about half of the spaces today are purchased in advance of death, and in many cases large family plots are purchased. Generally speaking, it is a good idea to view the cemetery and space before you purchase it; after all it will be your final resting place. It will also be the place where your family and friends come to pay their respects to you so you should ensure that it can be easily accessed.

There are two general types of cemeteries in the United States and Canada:

(i)   a traditional monument cemetery; and

(ii)   a type of memorial park in which the only grave marker that can be used is a bronze marker set flush with the ground.

You should consider which type of cemetery you would like to be interred in.

The price of a plot in a cemetery varies from approximately $250 for a single plot in a small town to $3,000 in a larger city or town. You will need to telephone the operators of the cemetery in question or visit the cemetery in order to confirm the exact prices. You will also need to have made a decision in terms of what you want to purchase. In addition, to the direct cost of the grave there may be other costs such as those commonly applied for the opening and closing of the grave. These charges may recur when family plots are reopened and reclosed. In some instances, the cost for opening and closing a grave can be as much as, if not more than, the original cost of the plot. So be sure to check this out when purchasing a grave especially a family plot.

Many cemeteries have rules and regulations relating to the use of grave markers and monuments, as well as planting restrictions around the grave itself. As such, it's a good idea to make inquiries about these issues before you make a decision to purchase your plot.

When selecting a cemetery it may also be a good idea to check whether the cemetery has a properly functioning maintenance policy or whether your family will be responsible for the grave's upkeep. Where there is a maintenance policy in place, there may be an annual upkeep fee for this service. This will need to be discharged by family members. However, you shouldn't just accept the word of the cemetery operators that a maintenance policy is in place. Have a look around the cemetery and see for yourself. A quick inspection will give you a good indication of the level of service. Remember, as this may well be your final resting place you will want it to be maintained and kept respectable.

When choosing a cemetery space or plot, you should consider the following issues:-

- the cost of the plot itself;

- the costs associated with the opening and closing of the grave;

- the cost of any annual maintenance fee;

- the cost of an outer burial container, liner or vault (see below);

- the cost of a marker or headstone and any restrictions which might apply to its erection (see below);

- whether a burial permit is required and has been issued in relation to the plot;

- whether there is any relationship between the cemetery and your funeral service provider - this may allow for a discounted transportation fee between the two locations;

- the future growth and development plans for the cemetery;

- that the advance purchase of a space or plot will probably make it less expensive in the long run;

- that the advance purchase of a space or plot will ensure that you can be buried near to your loved ones and, in time, they can be buried close to you.

You can generally purchase a plot through the cemetery, cemetery property re-sales, funeral service providers, brokers, or ads in the newspaper. Your funeral service provider should be able to give you more details of how to go about purchasing the plot. Alternatively, if there is a full time operator of the cemetery you can telephone or visit them. There are also a few sites on the internet which sell pre-owned plots. You should browse through some of these sites as they could give you a good indication of the prices in your area.

Grave Liners and Burial Vaults

A grave liner or burial vault is a type of container that is placed in a grave before burial. It serves to create an outer shell around a casket which prevents the ground from sinking when the casket deteriorates. It is usually made of concrete or bronze.

The main difference between a grave liner and a burial vault is that the former usually only covers the top and side of the casket whereas a burial vault encases the entire casket. In addition, burial vaults tend to be stronger and more expensive than grave liners. In fact, burial vaults are generally sold with a warranty as to their durability and fitness for purpose.

In reality, very few states require graves to be fitted with grave liners or burial vaults in order for burial to take place. However, the rules and regulations of many cemeteries do impose such requirements. This is because the use of these items serves to aid the upkeep and maintenance of the cemetery by preventing graves from sinking. The requirement is therefore a fair one. If you wish to chose burial as an option, you should therefore check with your preferred cemetery to see if these types of protective containers are required. If they are, and you are not willing to purchase them, you may have to look around for a cemetery that doesn't require them.

It should be remembered that while grave liners and burial vaults prevent the ground from collapsing, they do not prevent the eventual decay of the deceased's remains.

The prices of grave liners and burial vaults vary widely. Grave liners tend to cost between $200 to $600 depending on their size and the materials used. Burial vaults, on the other hand, vary wildly in price from as little as $200 to $10,000 or more. The average purchase price for a burial vault is more realistically in or around $600. Grave liners and burial vaults can be bought from either a funeral service provider or from the cemetery itself so feel free to contact them to check out their prices.

Picture provided courtesy of memorials.com

Headstones and Markers

Purchasing a headstone can be a little overwhelming given the variety of different types of headstones available. They come in different shapes, sizes and colors; and are even cast from different materials such as bronze, granite or marble. They also vary in style and design. You can buy grave markers, upright headstones, angel headstones, child headstones, memorial pictures, memorial benches and so on. The choices are endless. So where do you start?

Well, if you have already decided where you would like to be buried, the first place to start will be with your chosen cemetery. Many cemeteries have strict rules regarding the types of headstones that they'll permit onto their burial grounds. These rules can relate to the size of the headstones as well as their color and style. For example, it's not uncommon for cemeteries to only permit certain colors of granite to be used on a granite headstone. If your headstone does not meet with the cemetery's requirements, the cemetery can refuse to allow its erection when the time comes. Therefore, your first step should be to make sure that the headstone or marker that you purchase conforms to the rules of your chosen cemetery. Needless to say, you should not buy a headstone without doing this simple check in advance.

Once you know what types of headstones are permitted in your chosen cemetery you can start your search for a headstone. The first thing to do will be to find a reputable headstone provider. You can either search for a provider on the internet or visit a number of different providers in the locality. Your funeral director should be able to give you a list of reputable providers in the area.

As you will probably not need the headstone for a number of years, it's important to make some assessment as to whether the provider will be in business in 10 or 20 years time when the headstone is needed. This is especially important where you pay in advance for the headstone. You should check to see how long the provider has been in business, what their reputation is like in the market place, has there been any complaints lodged against the provider with the Better Business Bureau, do they have a physical address, and so on.

The alternative to pre-paying for your headstone is to leave some money aside in a designated account that can be used to pay for your headstone and other funeral costs when the time comes.

Once you have sourced your headstone or marker provider, you can consider the type of headstone or marker that you want. The provider will be able to show you the various different designs and sizes offered. In addition, you could also take a look around the local cemetery to give you some ideas which might help personalize the stone. If you go with a customized design it will most likely cost you a little extra.

The price of headstones and markers start at about $500 and $100 respectively with the average prices coming in at around $2,000 and $1,000 respectively. In addition to the price of the headstone itself you will also need to consider the price of installing the headstone at the grave site. In many cases, the cemetery will have the headstone or marker installed for a fee. If they do not provide this service they (or your funeral service provider) will be able to direct you to a local monument installer who can assist. You should check with the cemetery about installation fees as you will need to factor these costs into your overall funeral plan.

Finally, some cemeteries require the completion of a number of forms before a headstone can be placed at a grave site. These forms typically request details of the size, color and type of headstone which is to be placed and may even require a drawing. The company from which you are purchasing the monument should be able to assist you with the completion of these forms. If not, the cemetery managers will most likely be able to assist.

 Did You Know?

It is illegal for a cemetery to refuse to allow you place a headstone merely because it was not purchased from the cemetery management company. If you are faced with such a problem, contact the Federal Trade Commission who will be able to assist you.

In summary, when shopping around for a headstone you will need to consider the following:-

- The type of headstones and markers allowed in the cemetery (example: upright headstones, flat bronze grave markers, flat granite grave markers, side by side companion, double interment grave marker, and so on).

- The minimum and maximum sizes allowed for cemetery headstones?

- Do any color restrictions apply to headstones or markers?

- Are there any other particular specifications that the cemetery requires?

Some cemeteries require lawn mower proof edges for the base of granite headstones, specific size requirements for the base, that a Christian symbol be incorporated into the memorial design and so on. Get a copy of the cemetery rules and check out the requirements.

- Is a permit needed to place a headstone? Some cemeteries require that permits be issued before headstones or markers can be placed. This is to ensure that a suitable headstone or monument is added and that the plot owner or next-of-kin approves of the placement. Again, you will need to inquire about this directly with the cemetery management company.

- Will there be an installation fee for placing the headstone?

Entombment in a Mausoleum - An Alternative to Burial

Mausoleums have been in use since approximately 350 BC when they were first used to house the bodies of deceased Egyptian kings. A mausoleum is essentially a building which has been built for the specific purpose of housing the remains of one or more deceased persons after they have passed away. The bodies themselves are stored above ground in the mausoleum in defined burial spaces known as crypts.

Did You Know?

One of the most famous mausoleums in the word is the Taj Mahal!

Once a casket has been placed in a crypt, a granite or marble front is used to seal off the crypt. A form of plaque is then placed on the outside of the crypt to identify the person who has been entombed – somewhat like a grave marker.

There are a number of advantages to choosing entombment as opposed to traditional burial. These include the following:-

- As mausoleums are above ground, they tend to be cleaner and dryer than underground burial sites. This is something that appeals to many people.

- The cost of a crypt is comparable to the cost of a traditional burial plot especially when the expense of a graveside monument is taken into account. On average, crypts can be secured for between $2,000 and $4,000 depending on the location.

- Mausoleums reduce the amount of land used for burial – something which would appeal to those who are green at heart.

Crypts can come in various sizes and types. In most cases, crypts will be used for single entombments and layered 5 or 6 crypts high (of course this varies). However, it is also possible to have double crypts which can facilitate the entombment of two bodies in the same crypt. Double crypts come in three basic kinds:

- Tandem crypts which accommodate two entombments lengthwise in one crypt.

- Companion crypts which accommodate two entombments side by side.

- Westminster crypts which accommodate one entombment above ground and another below.

Like traditional grave plots, crypts can be purchased either at the time of death or in advance. Needless to say, if you wish to have your remains entombed in a particular mausoleum you may wish to purchase your crypt in advance. This will not only ensure that your wishes can be adhered to but will also remove some of the burden of funeral planning from your family following your death.

The entombment fees – the actual cost of opening and closing the crypt after your body has been placed in it - may also be pre-paid. If the fees are not pre-paid, they will become payable at the time of entombment.

It is important to note that mausoleums have strict rules in relation to the types of plaques that can be added to the outside of the crypt as well as the floral arrangements that can be laid out in front of the crypt. You should read these rules and regulations carefully before purchasing your crypt and adhere to them strictly in organising any funeral service.

Finally, it's worth mentioning that some crypts can actually be located underground such as underground lawn crypts or underground crypts in religious houses. Your local funeral provider will be able to give you full details of the options available to you in your locality.

Home Burials

Unsurprisingly, given the recent economic downturn, the number of home funerals taking place in the United States has increased dramatically over the last 5 years. In fact, there are now almost 50 organizations nationwide which assist people with home funerals compared with only two such organizations in 2002.

Home funerals typically involve the laying out of the deceased's body at home following death and the subsequent burial of the deceased on nearby land usually owned by the deceased or the deceased's family.

There is of course a raft of rules and regulations applicable to home burials in each state. However, with the help of organizations that provide home funeral assistance and 'death mid-wives' as they are known, the path to a home funeral is certainly a lot clearer than it once was. In most cases, they will be able to guide you through the home burial process without the need to engage a funeral service provider. However, in states such as Connecticut, Indiana, Louisiana, Michigan, Nebraska and New York, the law requires that a funeral director be involved in the handling of the deceased's remains at some point. In the remaining 44 states and the District of Columbia, the deceased's family can bury the deceased themselves.

In terms of formalities, families are typically required to obtain a death certificate evidencing the deceased's death and, if required, a burial transit permit so that the body can be moved from a hospital or funeral home to a cemetery, burial site or crematory. There may be other requirement such as having a specific amount of land or demonstrating how the grave site is to be maintained in perpetuity.

The costs of home burials are much less than traditional burials which cost about $6,000 on average. In fact, even in states where a funeral director is required to assist in the process, home funerals are still far less expensive than traditional funerals. There are a number of reasons for this:-

- Embalming is not required by law in any state in the United States. However, if you are having a home burial you will need to consider how the body will be kept cool and how do deal with other after death matters (such as fluid and gas leakage).

- There is no requirement in any state in the United States for a coffin or casket to be used for burial. This allows family members to use shrouds or even less expensive pine boxes for burial purposes.

- As the burial site is often family owned land, the cost of a grave in a cemetery as well as the related costs of grave liners, burial vaults and expensive headstones can be removed.

- Death midwives typically only charge $200 to $300 for consultation; although this can rise significantly depending on the mid-wife's schedule of fees and whether there is any travel involved. Compare this to the likely cost of a funeral director!

In most cases, it's likely that you will need assistance with preparing for a home burial. In this instance your local funeral director, doctor, minister of the faith, a death mid-wife and/or some of the home burial organizations mentioned above should be able to assist you.

Resources

- Home Funeral Directory – directory of home funeral service providers - www.homefuneraldirectory.com

- Crossings – information and workshops to assist with home funerals and green burials - www.crossings.net

- Final Passages – green and family directed funerals for California - www.finalpassages.org

- U.S. Funerals Online – funeral planning and online directory - www.us-funerals.com

- Casket Online - Discounted Caskets Online - www.casket-online.com

Green Burial

The Problems With Traditional Burial

The environmental problems relating to natural burials emanate from two principal concerns namely the use of embalming fluid in preventing decomposition of the body and the use of certain materials in the construction of coffins and caskets which are not environmentally friendly.

Embalming fluid is considered to be an environmental concern for two reasons. Firstly, embalming fluid contains a chemical substance called formaldehyde which is known to pose health risks to funeral home workers – hence the need to wear protective equipment when handling the substance. Secondly, the long term effects of formaldehyde on soil, soil organisms and air quality following the burial or cremation of bodies have not yet been determined. This is particularly worrying considering that approximately one pint (500ml) of embalming fluid is used per 6.35kg weight of the body. Worse still, the Casket and Funeral Association of America estimates that 827,060 gallons of embalming fluid (which most commonly includes formaldehyde) is placed into cemeteries in the U.S. each year.

Did You Know?

No state in North America compulsorily requires embalming of a body and, in fact, many expressly allow substitutes such as refrigeration or chilling of the body.

Coffins and caskets, on the other hand, pose their own types of environmental risks particularly where they are made from materials which are not biodegradable such as bronze, iron or steel. In fact, it is estimated that approximately 80% or more of the coffins sold in the United States in 2006 were made of steel. Even where the caskets are made of biodegradable materials such as wood, they may still contain some non-biodegradable elements such as glues, brass handles and so on. On top of all this, these environmental concerns are compounded by the fact that most cemeteries require the use of concrete or steel vaults or grave liners in graves to prevent the ground from sinking after the coffin has degraded.

Did You Know?

Each year, 22,500 cemeteries across the United States bury approximately:

- 30 million board feet (70,000 m³) of hardwoods (caskets)
- 90,272 tons of steel (caskets)
- 14,000 tons of steel (vaults)
- 2,700 tons of copper and bronze (caskets)
- 1,636,000 tons of reinforced concrete (vaults)
- 827,060 gallons (3,130 m³) of embalming fluid which most commonly includes formaldehyde.

(Compiled from statistics by Casket and Funeral Association of America, Cremation Association of North America, Doric Inc., The Rainforest Action Network, and Mary Woodsen, Pre-Posthumous Society)

The potential environmental effects of placing these materials into the ground on a continuous basis are plain for everyone to see.

What Is Green Burial?

In recent years, environmentally conscious people have favoured a number of alternatives to traditional burial and cremation. One such alternative which is increasingly being favoured by Americans is green burial. In fact, green burial has exploded in popularity over the last five years with the amount of green burial sites in the U.S. increasing exponentially over that time.

Green burials, or direct burials as they are also known, are burials which are carried out in an environmentally friendly manner. Its aim is to return the body to the earth in a way that does not restrict it from decomposing naturally and in a way that does not pose future hazards to public health. In line with these aims, the deceased's body is prepared for burial without the use of chemical preservatives or disinfectants such as embalming fluid which inhibits decomposition. It is then placed in either a shroud or in a biodegradable casket made from natural materials like willow, bamboo, or paper. Once the body has been prepared for burial, the shroud or casket is then placed in a shallow grave usually about three feet deep. The grave is kept shallow to aid natural decomposition and does not use a burial vault or outer burial container.

Green burials often take place in special reserves set aside specifically for green burials. In most cases, the burial site will be located in open woodland or in the countryside with trees, shrubs and flowers planted nearby and indeed often over the body itself so that it becomes part of the green environment. For example, in the Ramsey Creek Preserve, near Westminster, South Carolina 32 acres of land have been set aside for green burials and between five and ten people are interred there each year. As with traditional cemeteries, careful records are maintained of the precise location of each burial site, sometimes using GPS (global positioning system) devices.

In selecting a green burial site, be sure to visit the site in advance and check with the site providers as to the future plans for the area and the certificates it has to ensure that the ground remains a green burial site into the future. Remember, do your homework!

Costs of Green Burial

The funeral costs of a green or direct burial are likely to be much less than a traditional service. This is for a number of reasons. Firstly, as the body will not be embalmed, the funeral provider's costs will be reduced. Secondly, the cost of a biodegradable casket or shroud will typically be a lot cheaper than say an immaculately finished wood or metallic casket. Thirdly, the cost of a green burial site is likely to be significantly cheaper than a cemetery plot – especially as you will not need to buy a grave liner or vault. Fourthly, as only a small marker will mark the burial site, there will be no need to incur the cost of expensive headstones.

Similar to traditional funerals, there will be a small fee incurred for the opening and closing of the grave.

Of course, if you wish to have some form of funeral ceremony, it may be possible using environmentally friendly embalming fluid or by having your body refrigerated in advance of the ceremony. Your funeral provider will be able to advise you on the options available to you. Needless to say, if you have any form of funeral service you will need to take account of the associated costs – as pointed out in relation to traditional burials.

One thing worth mentioning in the context of funeral ceremonies for green burials is that the location of the site will have an important impact on the transportation of the body to the site, people's ability to visit the site and the type of ceremony that can be conducted at the site. So bear this in mind if the green burial site is located half way up a mountain!

To give you a flavour of the typical costs of a green burial, we have listed below the 2010 prices adopted by the Ramsey Creek Preserve (as listed on their website).

Traditional Natural Burial
$2,500 to $3,500 - depending on location
Includes free stone marker and a variety of native plants for the grave site

Burial of Cremated Remains
$550 to $1,050 - depending on location
Includes free stone marker and native plants for the grave site
(Note: This does not include the cost of transportation and funeral home fees.
Those arrangements need to be made separately with a funeral home.)

Additional Costs
Opening and closing of the grave: - $300 to $500.
Family and friends are welcome to assist if they choose.
(This fee does not apply to the burial of cremated remains.)
Engraving of marker: - Whatever the engraver charges.
Average prices range from $85 to $200.

Memorials

Ramsey Creek offers a variety of memorials including:
restoration fund for the renovation of the All Faiths Chapel;
memorial Stained glass windows;
benches and seating areas in the preserve; and
plantings of trees, shrubs and wildflowers.

Considerations for Family & Loved Ones

While the environmental and financial benefits of a green burial might be very appealing, you should also consider the bereaved before deciding on a green burial. This is because the traditional funeral format is a familiar recognition of death which allows friends and families of the deceased to come to terms with a death and to commence the grieving process. Green burials, on the other hand, often don't allow for viewings of the body or even traditional funeral ceremonies as the body is generally buried quite quickly following death (due to the restriction on using embalming fluid to preserve and conserve the body).

Burials at Sea

Burial at sea describes the process of disposing of a body by dropping it from a boat or ship in to the sea. Historically, it took place quite frequently during long sea voyages as the threat of disease often forced ship captains to dispose of the body swiftly while still at sea. This generally involved wrapping the body in a shroud and then throwing it overboard.

In modern times, however, the reasons for sea burial are far less dramatic. In most cases, people choosing to have sea burials will have very close links to the sea usually through activities like diving, fishing, surfing, swimming, yachting, etc. Others may have spent their lives in the navy. Of course, everyone has a different reason for choosing a sea burial.

When it comes to sea burials, there are of course strict rules and regulations which apply. For example, the Environmental Protection Agency regulations for full body burials at sea in the United States require that the site of internment be three nautical miles (3.5 miles or 5.6 km) from shore and in water at least

600 feet (180 m) deep. However, certain areas, including east central Florida, the Dry Tortugas, Florida and west of Pensacola, Florida to the Mississippi River Delta, require water at least 1,800 feet (550 m) deep. You will need to get a permit from the local state agency for full body burial and also notify the EPA within 30 days of committal of the body to the sea. Interestingly, full body sea burials are not permitted in the state of California.

The extensive depth is required to ensure that the body cannot be swept ashore by currents or tides. Given the necessity to adhere to the required depth, it may be necessary to travel a considerable distance offshore to find a suitable location. In fact, in some areas of the northeastern United States this may require travel in excess of 30 miles (48 km) for a suitable location!

Sea Burial Costs & Services

Like all funerals, the cost of a sea burial will be determined by the services and products that you require. In the first instance, you will need to engage the services of a traditional funeral director and/or a maritime funeral director. They will arrange any viewing services or ceremonies that you require and also prepare the body for burial. For viewings, you may need to rent a casket from the funeral provider as the body will ultimately be placed in a special marine casket, weighted body bag or a piece of sailcloth for burial.

You will also need to factor in the cost of the vessel and crew for the service. Again, the cost here will vary based on the size of the vessel, the number of staff required to operate it, the number of people that will be travelling on the boat and the destination.

Resource

New England Burials at Sea LLC Price List 2010

- Unattended Ash Scattering: $395 – Photo journaled Captain's service without family.

- 1 – 6 Passengers: $895 – $995 - Private cruise (2-3 hours)

- 7 – 35 Passengers: $1,750 – $3,150 - Private cruise (2-3 hours)

- 36 – 110 Passengers: $2,750 – $4,950 - Private cruise (2-3 hours)

- 110+ Passengers: approx $4,800 – $7,950 - Private cruise (2-3 hours+)

The type of service you require will also be a factor in determining cost. In this respect, you can typically choose to have a service held on the boat at the time of burial or on the pier immediately prior to departure. Alternatively, you can simply have the funeral provider give the body to the sea without the presence of too many family or friends and hold a memorial service at a later date. The choice is yours to make.

In relation to the services themselves, it should be remembered that the weather will play a key role in determining whether the service can take place and how it takes place. Rough sea conditions not only restrict long services but can also make people quite sick particularly when the vessel is required to travel a considerable distance to facilitate the burial.

Navy Burials

The United States Navy facilitates sea burials for certain eligible people including active-duty members of the uniformed services, retirees and honorably discharged veterans, U.S. civilian marine personnel of the Military Sealift Command and dependent family members of the foregoing.

The ceremony itself is performed while the ship is deployed at sea and, as a result, civilian family members and friends of deceased are not permitted to attend. However, arrangements can be made to have the service video taped.

The service is often divided into a military portion and a religious portion. The military portion involves the stopping of the ship (where possible), the lowering of the flags to half mast, an assembly on deck, a bugler, the placing of the casket on a stand at the side of the ship, and the covering of the coffin with a flag. A brief religious ceremony is performed by the ship's chaplain or commanding officer depending on the deceased's faith. Once the ceremony has concluded, the casket bearers tilt the stand on which the casket is resting thereby allowing the casket to slide overboard into the ocean. The flag which was draped over the casket is retained. A firing party then fires three volleys and the bugler commences playing "Taps". In addition, flowers or petals are often dropped into the ocean at the committal site.

Once the committal service has concluded, the commanding officer of the ship assigned to carry out the ceremony will notify the family of the date, time, and longitude and latitude of the service.

Finally, it's worth mentioning that it's also possible to have ashes scattered at sea as part of the ceremony rather than having a full body sea burial.

For specific details on the requirements of naval burials and how to arrange one simply visit http://www.navy.mil/navydata/questions/burial.html. Alternatively, if you have any questions about the naval burial at sea program, you can contact the United States Navy Mortuary Affairs Office Casualty Assistance Branch at Naval Personnel Command (NPC-621), 5720 Integrity Drive, Millington TN 38055-6210, Toll Free: 1-800-368-3202.

The Difficulty With Sea Burials - Memorials

One of the main problems associated with sea burials is that the family of the deceased are often left with no fixed place to mourn their departed loved one. They have no gravesite to attend and no place to pay respects to their loved one. This can often make it difficult for them to come to terms with the death. As such, you should give careful thought to this before settling on a sea burial. Separately, you might consider it appropriate to erect a small memorial some where that will give your loved ones this place of reference for your life.

Resource

- New England Burials at Sea –North East Sea Burials Provider - www. NewEnglandBurialsAtSea.com

- Sea Services – Nationwide Maritime Funeral Providers - www. seaservices.com

- Nature's Passage – Burial at Sea Service Provider - www.naturespassage. com

- Veteran's Funeral Care – Sea Burial for Veterans - http://www. veteransfuneralcare.com/veteransfuneralhome/burialAtSea.cfm

- Environmental Protection Agency Regulations - http://www.epa.gov/ region4/water/oceans/burial.html

- Navy Burials at Sea - www.navy.mil/navydata/questions/burial.html

Cremation

Cremation is an increasingly popular alternative to burial or entombment. It involves placing the body (which is enclosed in some form of outer container – see "Caskets for Cremation" below) in a cremation chamber for approximately 2 hours where, through a combination of both heat (at temperatures between 760 to 11500C (1,400 to 2,1000F)) and evaporation, the body is reduced to ashes and bone fragments. The remains are then placed into a crushing device which grinds the remaining fragments of bone in to a fine, sand like material. The cremation process can take up to 5 hours to complete but once it has been completed, the remains of the body (known as "cremains") are placed in an urn or temporary container to facilitate the transport of the remains to their final resting place.

As mentioned earlier in this chapter, choosing cremation does not rule out the option of having a funeral service. In much the same way as the traditional burial service, your body can be put on display in a funeral home or church and you can undergo the same religious ceremonies. The main difference is that the actual burial element is most often removed.

How to Choose a Crematorium

The vast majority of funeral providers don't actually have their own crematoriums. As such, in the majority of cases the cremation element of the funeral process will be contracted out to a third party crematorium. Usually, the funeral provider will have a preferred crematorium that they usually work with. Of course, if you are opting for a direct cremation without the use of a funeral service provider you will be able to approach crematoriums directly. Although remember that in a few states a funeral provider is required to handle the body (see the section on Home Burials above).

In approaching a crematorium, there are a few things you need to consider and a few questions you should ask:

- Check to see if the crematorium is state regulated and insured; and whether it has certification by The Cremation Association of North America (312-644-6610 or www.cremationassociation.org).

- Check to see if any complaints have been registered against the crematorium in the local Better Business Bureau (www.bbb.org).

- Request proof of frequent state inspections. Appropriate certificates are usually prominently displayed.

- Ensure that the staff is understanding and attentive.

- Enquire about body tracking procedures to ensure that there is no possibility of a mix up of the remains.

- Check out prices lists and customer testimonials (if any).

- See if you can view the facilities and enquire about the cremation process and timings.

While the above tasks may seem a little tedious, it's a small price to pay to know that your remains will be properly treated and that your family will be properly cared for during a difficult time.

Cremation can be a good option for those that don't like the thought of leaving their bodies to decompose deep down in the earth. However, before deciding on cremation particular attention must be paid to religious beliefs. For example, the Greek Orthodox and Orthodox Judaism faiths disapprove of cremation while the Roman Catholic and Protestant faiths take a more open view in approval of it. If you have any doubts as to whether your faith permits cremation, speak to a minister of your faith.

In addition, for those of you that are environmentally conscious, it's important to remember that, as mentioned previously in the section on green burials, cremation may not exactly be environmentally friendly. This is because the burning of certain chemicals found in embalming fluid and the use of fossil fuels – which produces carbon - to facilitate the cremation itself all adversely affect the environment. So, don't make the mistake of thinking that your cremation will be environmentally neutral! However, many believe that the environmental damage caused by traditional burial far outweighs that caused by cremation – especially as many crematoriums have taken measures to reduce the emissions which are caused by the cremation process. The debate on this continues however.

Caskets for Cremation

If you opt for cremation instead of burial, you will need to consider whether you wish to purchase a casket outright or simply rent one from your funeral service provider. The cost savings from renting generally presents an advantage when compared to the cost of purchasing a casket outright.

Where you choose to rent a casket, it will typically be made available during visitation times and during any required funeral services. Once all of these ceremonies have concluded, your remains will be transferred into an appropriate casket for cremation. This will usually be an in-expensive casket.

On the other hand, if you do not plan on allowing visitations or having any public viewing, the funeral service provider should be able to show you some simple casket options which are designed for cremations. In many cases, the cost of these caskets is often less than the rental charge for the visitation and ceremonial caskets. However, if you are very price sensitive, you can usually select an alternative container - made of pressboard, cardboard, or canvas - that is cremated with the body.

Whatever casket you choose, you will need to ensure that it is suitable for cremation. The majority of crematoriums require that the deceased's remains be either in a cremation casket or some other form of container. Needless to say, the container you choose should give a proper covering for the body and should afford an appropriate standard of respect and dignity.

The majority of crematories will not accept metal caskets. As such, if you wish to be cremated in a particular crematorium it would be wise to check out their requirements for cremation before you purchase your casket.

Picture provided courtesy of memorials.com

It is important to remember that the body will be cremated in the same enclosure that it arrives in when it comes to the crematorium.

Under the Funeral Rule, funeral service providers are prohibited from stating that state or local law requires a casket for direct cremations because none do. They are also obliged to inform you in writing that you can purchase an unfinished wooden box or an alternative container for direct cremation and actually make them available for direct cremation if you so require. The cost of caskets for cremation range from $300 upwards.

Cremation Costs

The costs of a cremation vary depending on the type of cremation you want as well as the products and services required of the funeral director. However, one thing that is certain is that, with an average price of less than $1,500, cremations are cheaper than traditional funeral services with burial.

Direct cremations for example can often cost less than $1,000. A direct cremation is where the deceased's body is cremated without embalming, public viewings or even a funeral service. In many cases, a simple cremation casket can be purchased for as little as $300 (or less if you wish to use cloth instead of a casket!). On top of that, the other expenses that are likely to be incurred are cremation fees (approx $175+), transportation fees (approx $100+) and the cost of an urn (approx $20+). An all round direct cremation package can cost as little as $500 or less. However, remember, that in some states it is necessary to involve a funeral director in the handling of the body (see section on Home Burials) and this will add to the cost of direct cremations. If no funeral director is required to handle the body, you will simply need to obtain a death certificate for the deceased and a transportation permit to bring the deceased to the crematorium (if you intend transporting the body yourself). In terms of commemorative services, where direct cremation takes place, memorial ceremonies are usually held at a later date.

Traditional cremations on the other hand tend to be more expensive than direct cremations. This is because all of the hall marks of a traditional funeral are included in traditional cremations such as the engagement of a funeral director (approx $750+), embalming (approx $350+), the transportation of the body to and from the funeral home (approx $100+), viewings, church ceremony, caskets for viewing (rentals from $200+), and an urn (approx $20+). All in all, traditional cremations cost about $1,500 on average with significant discounts often being offered on cremation packages. Of course, this price varies based on transportation distances, the casket chosen, the urn chosen and, of course, where you live – city crematoriums traditionally being more expensive than others.

Other additional costs may include refrigeration (approx $50 per day), transfer of ashes, disposal of ashes, burial of ashes, placement of ashes in a columbarium, etc.

You should check the precise prices with your preferred crematoriums and with online retailers. Remember, you don't need to buy all your products in one place!

Disposal Options After Cremation

In any event, once your body has been cremated there are a number of options available to you for the final disposition of your cremains. One of the most popular options is to have cremains placed in an urn. An urn is essentially a sealed vase with no handles. Once placed in an urn, the family of the deceased can decide what do to with the cremains. Typically they tend to either keep the ashes at home in an urn or have them scattered at a particular site. What the family does with the cremains will most likely be influenced by the deceased's wishes in that respect.

Types of Cremation Urns

There are various different types of urns that you can choose from. In addition to the different types of materials used in the construction of the urns, there is an array of different styles, themes and shapes to choose from. This variety will allow you to choose an urn that, in someway, is representative of your life or has personal meaning to you.

There are numerous different types of urns you can choose from including:-

* Themed Urns

  Themed urns are normally used when a family member wants to highlight a particular hobby, interest or sport. For example, a keen golfer may have an image of his favorite course placed on the front of the urn while a keen sailor may go one step further and have the urn constructed in the shape of his favorite yacht.

* Religious Urns

Religious urns typically showcase a person's faith or religious beliefs and are generally available in many different styles and materials.

- Keepsake Urns

Keepsake urns are smaller urns which are used to keep a small part of a deceased person's ashes. They are most commonly used where a deceased person's ashes are being divided between several family members or where the deceased's ashes are to be mostly scattered with a small portion being retained.

- Artistic Urns

Artistic urns are hand made urns cast from materials such as bronze, glass or ceramics. Because of their artistic quality and unique qualities, they usually command a high price.

- Biodegradable Urns

Biodegradable urns provide an environmentally friendly means of scattering cremated remains over land or out at sea. The materials from which biodegradable urns are constructed fully decompose over a short space of time. This allows the cremains contained within the urn to be gently released into nature in a non-intrusive process. For land burials, biodegradable urns are typically made of wood, paper or hemp and degrade over a number of weeks and months depending on the materials used to make the urn. In the case of bio-degradable sea urns, they typically float on the surface for a short period before sinking to the sea floor. Thereafter they usually degrade over a two to three day period thereby releasing the cremated remains to the sea.

- Companion Urns

These types of urns are designed to hold the cremated remains of two people in two separate compartments within the urn. They are intended to act as a symbol of the love and companionship between the two people whose remains it holds. They can come in a variety of shapes, designs and sizes.

- TSA Approved Urns For Travel

While you may think that travelling with an urn should be a relatively straight forward task, there can be complications especially if you are planning on travelling by plane. Due to the increased security measures put in place at most airports post 9/11 it has become more difficult to carry urns through airport security x-ray scanners. This has lead to many embarrassing moments and, of course, heated arguments! To avoid this problem, it is recommended that suitable TSA compliant urns be used for transporting a deceased person's remains as they do not repel x-rays at airport security scanners. These urns are typically made from x-ray friendly materials such as silk and can be purchased from online retailers such as www.EverlifeMemorials.com.

Resource

- Cremation Association of North America - International organization of over 1,200 members- http://www.cremationassociation.org/

- Internet Cremation Society - Links to over five hundred companies offering cremation-related items - http://www.cremation.org/

- FuneralPlan.com - Learn more about cremation and funeral options - http://www.funeralplan.com/funeralplan/cremation/

- Religious Tolerance – Cremation and Burial: Jewish & Christian Beliefs - http://www.religioustolerance.org/crematio.htm

- Cremation.com - Find local funeral homes and cremation providers in your area along with information and resources that can help you - http://www.cremation.com/

- International Cemetery and Funeral Association - international trade association for the cemetery, funeral, cremation and memorial industry - http://iccfa.com/

- Elegant Urns – Large Selection of urns - www.eleganturns.com/

- Stylish Funeral Urns – Traditional classic styled urns – www.stylish-funeral-urns.com

- Mainly Urns and Memorials – Large selection of urns - www.mainelyurns.com

- Memorials.com – Large selection of urns and other funeral products - www.memorials.com

- Cremation Solutions – Range of personalized urns - www.cremationsolutions.com

- In the Light Urns – Biodegradable and green urns - http://www.inthelighturns.com/biodegradable.html

Earth Burials

In much the same way as a casket is buried so too can an urn with your cremated remains. You will need to purchase a small plot in the cemetery for the burial as well as a burial vault and marker. You will also need to pay for the opening and closing of the grave. Your local funeral director of cemetery management company can advise you of your options and of the related costs. However, in reality they are much the same as those available for burials save the costs are a lot less due to the smaller amount of space required.

Above Ground Burials – Columbariums

If you wish to have your cremated remains buried above ground you can do so in a columbarium. A columbarium is a vault or wall with niches or cavities that has been built to store the remains of those who have been cremated. The urns are usually placed into these cavities and, in many instances, the cavities are then sealed. Generally, a small marker of some description is placed on the outside of the cavity.

The average cost of purchasing a cavity or niche varies from about $100 to $2,000 depending on the location of the columbarium. Again, your local funeral director or crematorium can advise you of the precise locations and costs included.

Scattering of Ashes

Another popular choice is to have your remains scattered over a particular place that has a meaningful significance for you. People often request that their remains be scattered on certain cherished grounds, on a certain body of water, on a golf course and so on. However, in some states there are some legal restrictions on where ashes can be scattered so you should check with your local crematorium or funeral director to see what restrictions may apply.

The scattering of ashes at a particular location will give your family and friends a place by which they can remember you. This can be of great benefit to them in the long run as they will have a place where they can go to feel close to you. However, you should give careful consideration to your selection of location. In particular, you will need to consider what's likely to happen to that location in the future – Is your favorite park or hillside likely to be dug up and developed? Are there restrictions on accessing your chosen area? Are there any factors which might make the area undesirable for you? These types of events could emotionally upset your family if they occur as they will destroy what they view as your final resting place. So be sure to check local development plans and with local authorities before you make your final decision on location.

When it comes to the scattering of ashes, people also choose options like having their ashes scattered from a plane, hot air balloon or even a boat. Some of these methods can be expensive so you will need to make some price enquiries before selecting a specific option. Scattering of ashes from planes and hot air balloons can cost anywhere from $200 upwards depending on the location of where you want your ashes scattered. We have already looked at the issues and costs of full body burials at sea and much the same applies to the cost of scattering ashes at sea– save that urns tend to be cheaper than marine caskets!

Scattering Your Ashes at Sea

Having your ashes scattered at sea usually involves dropping your ashes from a boat or plane or even from a cliff top. There are however restrictions on where ashes can be scattered and in most cases, you will need to travel at least three nautical miles from shore before scattering the ashes. You should also check with the requisite state agency or a local funeral director to see if any specific requirements apply in the locality where you intend having your ashes scattered.

In addition to scattering your ashes at sea, it is also possible to have your ashes committed to the sea in a bio-degradable urn. This will usually sink to the bottom of the ocean and later degrade - thereby releasing your ashes to the sea.

Other Ideas for Disposal of Ashes

We touched previously on the idea of environmentally conscious people opting for green burials for full body burials. Similar burial options are also available for those who have been cremated thanks to eco-forests. Eco-forests allow people to scatter ashes either freely in the forest (with some restrictions) or at the foot of a particular tree which can be purchased as a specific memorial for the deceased or for a group of deceased people. Cremains or ashes can also be buried using bio-degradable urns. There are numerous eco-forests in the U.S. with the main ones in Pennsylvania, New Jersey, New York, Virginia and North Carolina. For more details, check out the website www.ecoeternity.com/our-forests.html.

Picture provided courtesy of eternalreefs.com

As people are becoming more imaginative in their attempts to help the environment, green burials have moved beyond their 'traditional' preserves to other areas such as the ocean. For example, companies like Georgia based Eternal Reefs Inc are creating living memorials in the form of artificial ocean reefs to help restore fragile reef ecosystems. This is achieved by mixing a person's cremated remains with the reef material and then placing the end product in the ocean. This artificial reef attracts marine life and over time establishes itself as a new ocean reef, as well as a permanent "living memorial" to the deceased. For more information, check out Eternal Reefs' website at www.eternalreefs.com.

In Miami, a society called the Neptune Society has completed what they call "the Neptune Reef Project". The Neptune Reef Project is an amazing underwater man made memorial reef which houses urns, statutes and other keepsakes. It's expected that over time the remains of 100,000 people will be laid to rest here. Have a look at their site which contains plenty of information, photographs and videos: www.nmreef.com.

For prices starting in excess of $500, the website www.memorials.com will commission the world famous artist Mono to create a colourful painting using paint mixed with your ashes. This piece of modern art will have a special meaning in your home and will certainly be more appealing that simply having an urn sitting on a shelf!

Cremation Solutions Inc, a Vermont based company, will also mix your ashes with paint for the purpose of painting your portrait. It really does bring a new meaning to life like portraits! See www.cremationsolutions.com/Cremation-Art-Portraits-c125.html.

Have you ever thought about having your ashes blasted out of a firework? Probably not! However, if you're looking for something a little novel, that's exactly what companies like Angels Flight (www.angels-flight.net) and Heavens Above Fireworks (www.heavensabovefireworks.com) will do. They will arrange a special fireworks display for your memorial service and modify some of the fireworks to contain your ashes. Displays by Angels Flight start at about $4,000 while Heavens Above Fireworks, a UK based company, will sell the special fireworks to you so that you can conduct your own display. Firework prices start at £75 each while a mini-display is likely to set you back about £500.

And if fireworks just don't go high enough for you, get in touch with Celestis (www.celestis.com). For 'modest' fees of between $650 and $12,500 Celestis offer a number of packages which will send your ashes into space, have them deposited on the surface of the moon or even sent into deep space! You can even get your ashes brought back to Earth if you want! What's more, from as little as $54, you can even have a star named after you - see http://www.starregistry.com.

Of course, if space is a little too high for you (in terms of altitude or cost!) then you can opt to have your ashes disbursed by plane or hot air balloon. Air Legacy, a Colorado based company, offers ash scattering from an aircraft in areas such as Colorado, Kansas, Wyoming and Nebraska – see www.airlegacy.com.

Cremation Solutions Inc also offer some fascinating ways of disposing of your ashes. You can have your ashes made into jewelry, diamonds, garden rocks, snow globes, bird houses, candle sticks and much more. Simply visit www.cremationsolutions.com for more information.

A Florida based company called Eternal Ascent (www.eternalascent.com) will place your ashes in a five foot biodegradable balloon that is filled with helium and released into the air. The balloon travels to about 30,000 feet and there, due to the expansion of the air in the balloon and sub-zero temperatures outside of it, the balloon pops and your ashes are dispersed. The cost of the service ranges from about $1,000 to $2,000.

Finally, Illinois based company, Life Gem (www.lifegem.com), can turn your ashes into a diamond. The diamond, in turn, can be fashioned into any form of jewelry. But be warned, diamonds don't come cheap! Prices start at $2,600 and range right up to $25,000!

Resource

- Memorials.com – a one stop shop for your funeral needs! – www. memorials.com

- National Park Service – www.nps.gov

- Cremations.org – a website portal for cremations - www.cremations.org

- US Cremation Equipment – cremation directory - http://www. uscremators.com/

Conclusion

As you will have seen from the foregoing, there are many options available to you in relation to the disposal of your remains. Take your time in deciding what to do and take the time also to discuss your plans with close family members. When you have decided what you want to do, you will need to do some research in to the options available from cemeteries, crematoriums, funeral service providers, casket providers, urn providers, liner grave providers, headstone and marker providers and so on. Remember that you are not under any obligation to purchase all your required items from one place so do shop around and speak to the various different providers. Once you have done your research, you should insert your details in to your funeral plan.

CHAPTER 6:

CHOOSING YOUR FUNERAL PROVIDER

Chapter Overview

The choice of funeral service provider is one of the most important decisions that you will need to make when preparing your funeral plan. We'll look at some of the issues relating to the selection of funeral service providers in this chapter.

Chapter 6

CHAPTER 6

CHOOSING YOUR FUNERAL PROVIDER

Searching for a Funeral Service Provider

Once you have a rough idea of the type of funeral that you want to have, the next step will be to meet with some funeral service providers to discuss what you want and your options. These discussions will be useful because the funeral service providers will be able to give you their professional views on the feasibility and costs of the funeral that you would like to have. They will also be able to present you with options that you had not yet considered.

When it comes to selecting a specific funeral service provider, many people make their selections based on convenience rather than the range of products and services being offered. Often local providers are selected, especially providers that have been used by the family in the past. However, while there are advantages in choosing a provider that is close to you and one that you can trust, there may still be disadvantages particularly when it comes to price. If there are few providers in your locality and there is not stiff competition on price, you risk paying over the odds for your funeral service.

Like shopping for any expensive item, the best course is always to shop around and compare prices. When comparing prices, be sure to consider the total cost of all the items together in addition to the costs of items bought separately. Every funeral service provider will have a price list that includes all the items essential for the different types of arrangements it offers. This is required by law. Many providers offer packaged funerals that may cost less than purchasing individual items or services separately. Packaged funerals are permitted by law, as long as the price list of the individual items is also provided.

Important Note

When shopping for funeral products or services be aware that while there are many honest and reputable funeral planning homes that offer pre-arranged funeral planning services/products, there are also many companies offering overpriced and overvalued funeral plans who may even take your money with no intention of fulfilling their end of the bargain. Ask to see a valid business license and for recommendations from clients if you are in any doubt as to the trustworthiness of the service provider!

In comparing the different funeral service providers don't just judge them on price alone. You should also look at the quality of service they provide as well as the quality of products, the manner in which they operate, their levels of sensitivity and compassion, their reputation in the market and so on.

To locate funeral service providers, you can start with your local telephone directory. This will most likely list the majority of providers in your area. You can also search on the internet. Internet searches are generally quite good as they give you a lot of important information about the services provided and their related costs. Finally, you can also speak to family and friends to get their opinions on the various providers located in your area.

Once you have found a number of providers, you should consider setting up meetings with them to discuss your plans and options.

Comparing the Costs of Funeral Service Providers

When planning a funeral, there are two major financial considerations – the cost of the funeral itself and the cost of burial or cremation. We have covered the latter above so now we will focus in on the former.

Comparing the cost of like items is relatively straightforward – you simply get a price list and make a direct comparison. However, comparing the cost of a funeral package can be a little more difficult despite the fact that funeral service providers are obliged to provide you with an item by item break down of the price of the package. To help you understand and compare the various packages on offer, we have examined some of the main package fees below.

Basic Services Fee

The basic services fee includes services that are universal to all funerals, regardless of the specific agreement. This includes items such as fees for the initial consultation, funeral planning assistance, ensuring the necessary permits and certificates are obtained, holding the remains in the funeral home, and coordinating funeral arrangements with the cemetery, church or other third parties. This fee does not include charges for optional services or merchandise.

Additional Services

These are costs for services such as transporting the remains to the funeral home and place of final disposition; embalming; dressing the body; use of the funeral home or morgue for the viewing; use of equipment; staff for a grave side service; limousine or transport for the family of the deceased; a casket; outer burial container or alternate container; cremation or interment. All of these will be added to the basic service fee.

Extra Fees

On top of the additional services fees that you may be charged, the provider may also charge you for other goods and services that it buys on your behalf from outside merchants. This would include matters like the placing of obituary notices, the sending of acknowledgment cards, providing flowers, providing pallbearers, providing officiating clergy and musicians. Some funeral providers will charge you only the cost that they themselves incurred while others will add an additional service fee.

The Federal Trade Commission's Funeral Rule requires those who charge an extra fee to disclose that fact in writing to the customer (although it doesn't require them to specify the amount of the mark-up on the items) as well as disclosing the exact cost of the items in question for you. If the funeral provider is uncertain of the precise costs of these items during the consultation they should give you a written estimate of the likely costs.

Common Funeral Charges Explained

Caskets:

A casket or coffin is usually the most expensive part of any funeral. The casket is used to display and contain the remains of the deceased either for burial or cremation.

Clergy or Priests:

The clergy will be responsible for arranging and saying mass for the deceased. They typically charge a nominal fee for this service.

Cremation Fees:

This represents the costs of the actual cremation.

Death Certificate:

This is a certificate evidencing death. A death cert must be produced and registered before the deceased's body can be buried.

Embalming:

This involves carrying out restoration work on the body to enable the body to be publicly viewed. This service must be requested directly from the funeral home as it may not be included in your package.

Facility Use:

This refers to the use of the funeral home for public viewings or receptions after the funeral.

Flowers:

This relates to the provision of flowers at your funeral service. It may also include a service fee for the arrangement of the flowers.

Grave:

This is a tiny plot of land into which a person's remains are interred. It is used for both burial and cremation purposes. Often a person will purchase a grave or plot at the local cemetery and designate it as their final resting place. A plot may contain room for one or more graves.

Memorial Stationary: This includes all memorial stationary such as acknowledgement cards, memorial folders, prayer cards and church service folders.

Memorials/Headstones: These are stone monuments or metal markers placed at a graveside. Generally there is a charge for the monument itself and a further one for the actual installation of the monument.

Obituary Notices: Obituary notices are death notices that are placed in the local papers and on radio stations. Again, there may be a small charge for this.

Packaging/Shipping: This refers to any handling of the body outside of the normal funeral service. It applies, for example, where a body needs to be transported between two cities.

Preparation: These charges relate to the sanitation and dressing of remains prior to any funeral service. It is similar to embalming but merely cosmetic and does not involve internal fluid or gas removals. Generally this may be included in a funeral package but do check this.

Transfers: Depending on the ceremony chosen, your remains may have to be moved to and from different locations. These locations can range from the family home, hospital, morgue, funeral home, crematorium or the cemetery. There will be a cost associated with each transfer.

Urn: An urn is a container which holds the remains of a cremated body either on a permanent or temporary basis.

Vaults and Liners: Vaults and liners are outer burial containers which surround a casket and usually prevent the ground around the grave from sinking.

Typical Funeral Costs

The following are the main charges which you might encounter in your funeral plan:

- Basic services fee for the funeral director & staff

- Pickup of body

- Embalming

- Other preparation of body

- Casket options

- Outer burial container (vault)

- Visitation or viewing - staff and facilities

- Funeral or memorial service - staff and facilities

- Graveside service - staff and equipment

- Hearse

- Other vehicles

- Transporting the body to another funeral home

- Receiving body from another funeral home

- Cost of plot or crypt (if one is not already owned)

Typical Funeral Costs
• Perpetual care
• Opening and closing the grave or crypt
• Grave liner, if required
• Marker or monument, headstone or gravestone (including setup)
• Cremation
• Urn
• Niche

The Funeral Rule

The Funeral Rule, enforced by the Federal Trade Commission, makes it possible for you to choose only those goods and services you want or need and to pay only for those you select. The rule enables you to comprehensively compare costs and services from various funeral homes and in turn allows you to select the most appropriate funeral arrangements. However it must be noted that this rule applies to funeral homes and not to third party dealers of items such as caskets, headstones, urns and so on.

The Funeral Rule gives you're the right to:

- Purchase Only the Items and Services You Require

  You may buy items such as caskets and urns from suppliers other than your funeral service provider. You are not obliged to accept a package deal offered by a funeral service provider, although these may offer you better value for money. The funeral provider cannot refuse to handle a casket or urn you bought online, at a local casket store, or somewhere else — or charge you a handling fee for doing that.

- Obtain Direct Quotation

  Funeral directors must provide the price of specific items on request should you ask for them over the phone. If you turn up in person, the service provider must provide you with a full itemized price list before showing you any caskets or other products.

- Get a Written Itemized Quotation

  The quotation should break down the cost of the funeral plan which you have been quoted for on an item by item basis. The service provider is not however required to disclose its mark up on costs. However they should provide you with a general price list. Most funeral homes carry a separate casket price list. It is advisable that you ask for this list as the more expensive caskets may just be on display or included in the standard package.

Once you have agreed to purchase a funeral package, you will receive a bill from the funeral service provider. This should show you exactly what you are buying and paying for. The funeral home must give you a statement listing every good and service you have selected, the price of each, and the total cost immediately after you make the arrangements.

In most states it is possible to have a burial without embalming the body. There is no legal requirement for this in any state. However some states may require embalming or refrigeration of the body if it is not buried or cremated within a specific time frame or if it is crossing state lines. Some funeral homes allow for direct burial or immediate cremation which will not require any preservation methods to be used on the body. If you wish to have a public viewing of your body, you may have to undergo embalming as this is a requirement by many funeral homes for public viewing. You may ask the funeral home providers if they can provide private family viewing without embalming. If some form of preservation is a practical necessity, ask the funeral home if refrigeration is available.

Important Note

The Funeral Rule prohibits funeral service providers from:

- misrepresenting legal, cemetery or crematorium requirements;

- embalming a body without permission and then charging a fee;

- requiring the purchase of a casket for direct cremation;

- requiring consumers to purchase specific goods or services as a prerequisite to furnishing others; and

- engaging in deceptive or unfair practices.

Resources

Funeral Regulations & Planning Resources

- The Federal Trade Commission - http://www.ftc.gov/bcp/edu/pubs/consumer/products/pro19.shtm

- Funeral Consumers Alliance - http://www.funerals.org

- National Funeral Directors Association - http://www.nfda.org resources

- Funeral Consumer Guardian Society – calculate the cost of your funeral – http://www.funeralconsumer.org

Memorial Societies

There are a multitude of memorial societies currently operating in the United States. These memorial societies are not-for-profit organizations that have been set up to help consumers get the best deals possible when planning funerals. Membership of the societies (which often comes at the expense of a small once off payment) affords customers discounted rates for both funeral and cremation services as well as detailed information on funeral planning and price comparison surveys. Volunteers from these societies will often act on your behalf in negotiating prices. It is a valuable resource for anyone putting the time in to preparing their own funeral and who is a little cost sensitive.

The Funeral Consumers Alliance (FCA) is one such society and has over 400,000 members. As well as providing information on your nearest FCA branch, it also offers plenty of resources and information to members and non-members alike. Its website can be found at www.funerals.org.

Selecting a Funeral Service Provider

While you are not required by law to use a funeral service provider to plan your funeral or indeed to facilitate it when the time comes (except in Connecticut, Indiana, Louisiana, Michigan, Nebraska and New York), there are many practical reasons for doing so. Apart from the logistical and cost benefits, it should also be remembered that your loved ones will most likely be experiencing the emotional difficulties of dealing with your bereavement. Using the service of a professional funeral home can greatly relive and comfort those in mourning and will be of huge benefit to your family.

Having compared the services and costs of several funeral providers, you will almost be ready to make your selection. However, before doing so, there are some other final issues which you should consider. These include the following:

- What the Better Business Bureau says about the provider and whether or not they are ISO 9000 registered.

- Any online reviews or articles about the service provider and its service.

- The size of the funeral home and whether it will suit your requirements.

- The demeanour, manner and helpfulness of the staff – remember they will be the ones dealing with your family when the time comes in very traumatic and difficult circumstances.

- The location of the site.

Having made your plan and selected your provider, you can agree the specifics with your funeral service provider. If you wish, you can purchase some of the items in advance directly from the funeral service provider or from third parties. However, if you are considering purchasing items like caskets from third parties in advance, you need to consider the issue of storage and the availability of the item when needed. What if the company that sold you a casket does not open on a Saturday or Sunday and you pass away on a Friday night? Be sure to plan things carefully.

What to Do Next?

Once you have chosen your funeral service provider and prepared your funeral plan, the next step will be to discuss your wishes with your family and anyone else that you wish to participate in your funeral. Your family and friends may even have additional suggestions that you had not considered. Once you have completed your discussions and decided on a plan, you should proceed to fill out the forms contained in the back of this book. This will help ensure that your wishes are honored and understood when the time comes.

 Resource

Remember to tell your loved ones where your plan can be located when needed! For more information on electronic document storage we recommend visiting the Legal Vaults™ website at www.legalvaults.com.

CHAPTER 7:
FINANCING THE COST OF YOUR FUNERAL

Chapter Overview

No funeral plan will work unless you have some means of financing it. In this chapter, we'll look at some of the most common ways of doing that.

Chapter 7

CHAPTER 7

FINANCING THE COST OF YOUR FUNERAL

Paying for Your Funeral

Before embarking on your funeral arrangement plan it is important to consider the cost of your funeral. We have covered many of the individual costs in the preceding chapters and, by now, you may have even got a firmer indication of the likely costs from speaking to funeral service providers. As you will now know, funerals are expensive and will cost several thousand dollars. In fact, the average funeral cost is probably in or around $5,000 to $8,000. You will also know that no funeral plan is complete with considering how the funeral will be paid for.

Some funeral homes require payment in advance once arrangements have been decided upon, while others are more liberal and may offer some form of payment plan. There is one general exception to all this and that arises in relation to cremation where full payment in advance is often required.

Pre-payment of Service Fees

Funeral service providers will usually present you with various options for paying for your funeral. The most common form of payment simply involves the issuing of an invoice after your funeral has taken place. The invoice will usually need to be discharged within 30 to 60 days of your funeral taking place depending on the provider's credit terms.

Funerals can also be paid for in advance. In this respect, the main options include the use of trusts and funeral insurance. We'll discuss each of these options below.

Funeral Trusts

Funeral trusts are used to help people save money to discharge the future costs of their funeral. In brief, you simply set up a trust account in a bank and add funds on a periodic basis. When you pass away, the bank will release the funds to a designated beneficiary (often a funeral service provider) to pay for the cost of your funeral. In order to ensure that the funds are sufficient to cover the costs of your funeral you should enter into a contract with the funeral service provider which guarantees that the funeral will be provided at a fixed price. This should help avoid shortfalls arising from an increase in the cost of the funeral. The contract, often called a pre-need contract, should also specify who should pay any shortfall if one arises as well as set out where any surplus funds should be transferred if the trust funds more than cover the cost of the funeral. Your funeral service provider should be able to provide you with a pre-need contract. However you should read this contract carefully before signing it.

There are various matters to consider when establishing a funeral trust so it's a good idea to have the funeral service provider explain the various regulations which apply to their establishment.

Funeral Insurance

Funeral insurance is an increasingly popular option for funding funeral plans. Under the terms of the policy you can name a specific funeral provider as a beneficiary. When you die the insurance proceeds are paid to the provider who in turn uses them to discharge the cost of your funeral service. In order to regulate this payment you should also enter into a pre-need contact with the service provider. The contract, as mentioned above, will stipulate what should happen if there is a deficit or surplus of funds.

Funeral insurance polices can generally be purchased from an insurance broker or from the funeral service provider.

As an alternative to standard funeral insurance, you could also purchase 'final expenses' cover which is a little like life insurance. When you die the insurance proceeds will be paid to your estate. In turn, your estate can use these funds to discharge your funeral costs (which take precedence over many other debts of your estate).

Advantages of Pre-paying

There are a number of advantages to paying for your funeral in advance. One of the main advantages arises in connection with cost. By paying in advance, you can lock in the prices as they apply today rather than subjecting yourself to inflationary price increases over the long term. Remember, prices typically double every ten years.

When pre-paying for a funeral it's important to obtain some form of written guarantee from the funeral service provider that it will deliver the agreed services and merchandise for the agreed price if you pre-fund or pre-pay your funeral. What you are trying to avoid is a situation where your funeral doesn't take place for 20 years and the service provider seeks to increase costs!

Another cost advantage arises as a result of your ability to select what features you want included in the funeral package. By controlling what you want included in your funeral package you can remove the risk of your family paying excessively for unnecessary items following your death.

Pre-paying for your funeral will also take away both cost and organizational burdens from your family at a very difficult time. This can give you the peace of mind of knowing that your family will not have the trouble of worrying about these matters.

Important Note

It is important in the planning process that you understand the difference between pre-paying and prearranging. Both pre-paying and prearranging allow you to record your wishes, but only pre-paying reduces the financial strain by paying in advance.

Using Benefits to Pay for Your Funeral

If you don't employ at least one or more of the above mechanisms in order to discharge the cost of your funeral, the payment will have to come from your estate. However, given that much of your assets will be frozen during probate, there is a risk that your family may have to discharge the immediate costs from their own pockets. It is therefore important to consider whether your estate might be able to claim any benefits on your behalf to help discharge the costs of your funeral bill. We'll discuss some of these benefits below.

Social Security Benefit

Social Security benefits are available to cover any person who worked under the Social Security system. A lump sum benefit of $255 is payable towards funeral expenses provided there is a surviving spouse living with you at the time of your death or, if you have no such spouse, payment may be made to your minor children if they are eligible for monthly benefits. Social security benefits must be applied for within two years of death and are paid directly to the surviving spouse or children.

Veterans' Benefits

There are a number of different benefits which are paid to veterans. These include:-

- The Veterans' Association pays an allowance of up to $1,500 to the family of a veteran if the veteran's death was related to service in the defense forces.

- The Veteran's Association pays the cost of transporting the remains of a service-disabled veteran to the national cemetery with available gravesites nearest his or her home.

- The Veteran's Association pays $300 towards the burial and funeral expenses of veterans who, at time of death, were entitled to receive pension or compensation or would have been entitled to compensation but for receipt of military retirement pay.

- The United States Government provides headstones and markers for the graves of veterans and eligible dependents anywhere in the World which are not already marked.

The U.S. Department of Veteran Affairs provides a number of benefits to eligible veterans and their families following the death of a veteran. These rights extend to include a gravesite in any of the 131 national cemeteries with available space, opening and closing of the grave, perpetual care, a government headstone or marker, a burial flag, and a presidential memorial certificate, at no cost to the family. Some veterans and/or their families may also be eligible for burial allowances.

Cremated remains can be buried or inurned in national cemeteries in the same manner and with the same honors as casketed remains.

For full details of the benefits available to veterans visit the Department of Veteran Affairs website at http://www.cem.va.gov.

Other benefits may be available to veterans depending on the situation so it is advisable to contact the Veterans' Association to discuss your eligibility.

If you wish to use any of these benefits as a method of paying or part paying your funeral expenses, you should gather and store the necessary application documents in a safe place and ensure that those organizing your funeral are aware of your wishes and the location of these documents.

Other Benefits

Other benefits may also be available to cover funeral expenses such as retirement plans, or employer and club schemes. If you have made arrangements with such organizations to provide for funeral expenses you should document these arrangements and the contact details for the organization in question carefully in your funeral plan. Again, you will need to make sure that your family is aware of these arrangements and the location of all requisite papers.

Conclusion

It's important to take the time to both plan your funeral and plan for its payment. We have included a funeral planning worksheet which can be used in conjunction with this book to help you prepare your funeral plan. If you are in any doubt as to your options or choices, speak to a funeral director. They will be best positioned to help you.

Good luck with your planning!

CHAPTER 8:
THE IMPORTANCE OF ESTATE PLANNING

Chapter Overview

Estate planning is something that often takes place in tandem with funeral planning. We'll give you a brief overview of what's involved in this chapter.

Chapter 8

CHAPTER 8

THE IMPORTANCE OF ESTATE PLANNING

Introduction

In order to prepare a comprehensive funeral plan you aught to consider not only the funeral planning process itself but also the more general issue of estate planning.

In planning for death, many people sadly overlook the importance of preparing a good estate plan. An estate plan is essentially a group of legal documents such as wills, living wills, living trusts and powers of attorney that work together to provide for the management of your affairs if you become mentally incapacitated and for the distribution of your assets when you die.

What Is Estate Planning?

As alluded to in the introduction, estate planning is the process of planning for the management of your estate in anticipation of your incapacity and the disposition of your assets upon death.

Preparing an estate plan is undoubtedly one of the most important steps that you can take in order to ensure that your healthcare wishes are honored should you become incapacitated, and that your wishes regarding the transfer of your property on death are complied with.

While people traditionally believed that a will formed the pillar of a decent estate plan, more and more people now appreciate the value of a comprehensive estate plan. Such a plan includes relevant legal devices to transfer property, appoint guardians for children, reduce taxes, avoid probate, provide for the management of their financial affairs during times of incapacity and appoint agents to make healthcare decisions. A good estate plan should also contain details regarding funeral and burial arrangements. Irrespective of a person's age or the size of their estate, a good estate plan can accomplish each of these tasks.

For most people, understanding estate planning options can appear to be quite a demanding endeavor at first glance. However, as you will see later in this chapter, many of the estate planning techniques commonly used are relatively straightforward. We will explore some of these techniques in brief in the ensuing pages.

What's Included in Your Estate?

So where do you start when you are making an estate plan? Well, before you decide who you want to give your assets to, you must first determine what assets you actually have to give away. In other words, you need to know what your estate is!

Simply put, your estate comprises of everything you own - all your property and possessions, including cash, investments, insurance policies, real estate, valuables, cars, jewelry and so on. It also includes any liabilities that you might have such as mortgages, car loans, outstanding utility bills, credit card bills and so on. The total value of your estate is equal to the "fair market value" of all of your various assets less all of your debts.

The value of your estate is important when it comes to determining whether your estate will be liable to pay any estate taxes after your death.

How to Plan Your Estate

Once you know exactly what you have to give away, you will need to look at the various estate planning options that are available to and suitable for you. Fortunately, estate planning is not as difficult or as complicated as it is often made out to be. In most cases, it simply involves a detailed consideration of your situation in life and how you would like your affairs managed if you become incapacitated or how you would want your assets distributed in the unfortunate event of your death. Once you understand the options available to you, you should be able to answer these questions a lot easier. At that stage, you can use a number of devices and legal documents to put your estate plan in to effect.

Surprisingly, preparing the legal documents is often the easiest part of the process. The most difficult part for most people is actually deciding on what they want to include in their plan. This is because there are a variety of different issues to consider before finalizing your plan. At the very least, you must ask yourself (and illicit answers for) the following questions:

- what assets do I own and how much are they worth?

- how much debt do I have?

- whom do I want to give my assets to when I pass away?

- do I want to wait until I die before giving my assets away or would it be better if I did it sooner?

- who should I appoint to manage my assets if I am unable to do so due to ill health?

- who should I appoint to take care of my minor children if I become unable to care for them myself?

- who should make medical decisions on my behalf if I become unable to do so?

Of course, there are many other questions that can and should be asked. However, for the moment the questions above are probably enough to get you started on your journey to preparing your estate plan.

 Resource

For more information on estate planning see our book entitled "Estate Planning Essentials". See page 201.

Do I Need to Plan My Estate?

Many people often think estate planning is for the wealthy or simply believe that there is no need for them to have an estate plan – after all, they don't have much anyway. The reality is that anyone who has reached the age of majority in their state, has any assets which are important to them, or who has children should make an estate plan.

The fact is, whether your estate is large or small, there are many compelling reasons why everyone (with very few exceptions) should take the time to organize and plan their estate. For example, developing and implementing a good estate plan will ensure:

- that your assets will be managed during any period in which you are incapacitated;

- that someone you know and trust will be able to make medical decisions on your behalf in accordance with your specific instructions and wishes should you become incapacitated;

- that your assets will be disposed of as you would have wanted following your death;

- that your family and friends will not have to wait months or even years to receive their inheritance following your death;

- that your children will be properly looked after by a guardian of your choosing and not one appointed by a court; and

- much more.

When it comes to estate planning, one thing is certain. If you fail to plan ahead, a judge will make all of the above decisions for you. In making these decisions, the judge will look at your state's law and the predefined estate plan that applies for everyone who fails to plan for the distribution of their estate themselves. In essence, a court will appoint someone to make medical decisions on your behalf, dictate who receives your assets based on specific rules of inheritance (known as the rules of intestacy), appoint someone to look after your children and much more. What is worse, neither your wishes nor those of your family can override the decision of the court.

From the above, you can see that one of the most compelling reasons to prepare an estate plan sooner rather than later is control. If you have a proper estate plan in place then you, and not a court, can determine how your affairs are dealt with.

We will now take a brief introductory look at some of the various estate planning devices and techniques that you may need to use to implement your plan once you have finalised your thoughts in that respect.

Children and Guardians

If you are a parent, it is likely that your first priority will be to make proper arrangements for the future care of your children should you and your spouse or partner die before they grow up. You can do this by simply appointing a guardian who will be responsible for their care, welfare and education. A guardian can be appointed under the terms of a specific guardianship agreement or under the terms of your will.

Remember, if you fail to appoint a guardian for your children, the court will appoint one of its choosing. On the other hand, if you plan your estate in advance, you can be sure your children are well taken care of by people you know and trust.

Apart from the day-to-day care of your children, you will also need to consider who will have day-to-day responsibility for managing any inheritances they receive whether from you or from someone else. In many states, minor children are not allowed to own significant property or assets outright. As a result, it becomes necessary to appoint a property guardian or trustee to manage those assets on their behalf. A property guardian or trustee (while similar to each other) is different to a personal guardian in that they are only concerned with the management of the child's property and not specifically with the child's care, welfare or education. This remains the responsibility of the personal guardian. Often, the same person is appointed as personal guardian, property guardian and trustee. However, you may wish to separate the tasks, as many do, and assign them to those people you feel best qualify for the particular job in question.

Choosing Beneficiaries

Deciding on who will be entitled to receive your assets following your death can be an extremely rewarding and gratifying experience.

While many people simply choose to leave their estate to their spouse or children, the exact decision as to who will benefit from your estate and the manner in which your estate will pass to those beneficiaries will most likely be influenced by a number of important factors including whether:

- your intended beneficiaries are minors or adults? If they are children, you will most likely need to make arrangements to have someone manage their inheritance until they reach a specific age;

- you have any children with special needs? If so, you may wish to create a trust to provide for their long-term care?

- your beneficiary, irrespective of his or her age, is sufficiently capable of managing a large inheritance on his or her own or whether they need assistance? Again a trust may be considered;

- you wish to disinherit your spouse or child? If you do, there are only a limited number of ways in which you can do this!;

- you want to leave something to charity? If so, you could use tax efficient trusts to leave these gifts; and

- there will be tax implications associated with the giving of assets to a particular beneficiary? Again, tax can be deferred or, in some cases, avoided by the use of specific devices.

All of the above considerations, and more, will play a fundamental part in your choice as to who receives your specific assets and the manner in which they do so.

Last Will and Testament

A will, more formally known as a "last will and testament", is a legal document that allows you to express your desires and intentions with regard to the transfer of your real and personal property following your death. It allows you to put your wishes down "for the record" so that, should disputes or confusion arise, you may be assured that your intentions will be respected and followed after your death. Both statutory and common law (laws as interpreted by the courts) require that your heirs follow your documented wishes when determining how your estate is divided amongst them.

For those with sizeable estates, a will can play a strategic role in tax planning. The manner in which your property is passed, how much of it is passed and to whom it is passed determines how both the estate and the recipients of such property are taxed. A carefully drafted will can reduce estate and inheritance taxes, transfer costs and even the general costs of probate and administration.

Apart from prescribing how your property should be transferred to your loved ones following your death, a will is extremely flexible when it comes to managing property transferred to children. You can choose from a variety of property management options for children who are to receive property under your will. In addition, your will also affords you the opportunity to choose a personal guardian to care for your minor children after your death.

The terms of your will also usually dictate who will look after your affairs and take charge of carrying out your instructions following your death, including your sentimental, burial and memorial wishes. This of course is important as you will invariably want to ensure that the person managing your affairs (ie. your executor) will honor the various choices that you have made in your will.

The primary drawback of using a will is that it can take a number of months (and sometimes years) to complete the probate process – the formal process by which assets are transferred to the beneficiaries named in a will. This process often has the effect of slowing down the transfer of many of the estate's assets to the intended beneficiaries. To avoid this problem, there are numerous estate planning tools that can be utilized and we will discuss each of these further below.

Resource

For further information on wills, see our book entitled "Make Your Own Last Will & Testament". See page 198.

Revocable Living Trusts

A revocable living trust is a type of 'inter vivos' trust (i.e. a trust made between living people) used for estate planning purposes. Under the living trust arrangement you, as the creator of the trust, declare yourself trustee of the trust and then transfer some or all of your personal property to the trust. The legal ownership of the property passes from you personally to the trust. However, as trustee of the trust you maintain control over and use of the trust property.

As creator of the living trust, you can, at any time, either revoke the trust or call for the return of some or all of the property transferred to it. You can also add assets to the trust, change the terms of the trust and even make it irrevocable (incapable of change) at any time in the future.

After your death, the trust assets will pass to the beneficiaries that you have named in the trust document in much the same way that they would under a will. Specifically, your trust document will nominate a person known as the "successor trustee" (which is a little like an executor or personal representative) who will have the responsibility of transferring ownership of the assets in the trust to the beneficiaries named in the trust document following your death. In most cases, the whole transfer process takes only a few weeks.

From an estate planning perspective, one of the most important features to note is that since the assets in the trust are legally owned by the trust, they will not form part of your probatable estate at the time of your death. As such, there will be no need for any of these assets to go through the probate process; nor may those assets be available to settle debts from your estate (other than taxes which might be due). This, in turn, allows for the speedy distribution of those assets to the beneficiaries named in the trust document. Once all of the assets are transferred to the beneficiaries, the living trust ceases to exist.

Revocable living trusts are very easy to establish and manage and, apart from avoiding probate, there are many advantages to using living trusts as part of your overall estate plan. These reasons relate to the management of your assets during incapacity, privacy, tax and more.

 Resource

For further information on living trusts, see our book entitled "Make Your Own Living Trust & Avoid Probate". See page 198.

Executors and Probate

As briefly mentioned above, probate is the court supervised administrative process by which the assets of a deceased person are gathered, applied to pay debts, taxes and expenses of administration and then distributed to the beneficiaries named in the deceased's will. This process generally takes six to twelve months to complete, but where complexities arise it can last for years! In most cases, assets cannot or at least should not be transferred to the beneficiaries under the will until probate has been completed.

It follows, therefore, that where you make a will, you will also need to appoint an executor (otherwise known as a personal representative) to probate your estate following your death. Your executor will be responsible for handling, safeguarding and distributing your property in accordance with the terms of your will. In addition, he or she will also be responsible for ensuring that any debts or taxes owing by you at the date of your death are paid by your estate. These payments, if any, are often paid from the assets of the estate before any distributions are made to the beneficiaries named in a will.

Resource

For further information on executors and probte, see our book entitled "How to Probate an Estate - A Step-By-Step Guide for Executors". See page 199.

Assets that Don't Go Through Probate

If you have a spouse, child or other person that is financially dependent on you, they may need immediate access to funds from your estate in the event of your death. As such, you will need to consider how you can transfer some or all of your assets to them in a manner that will avoid a potentially long probate process.

This can be achieved in a number of ways. Firstly, you can avail of some of the probate free transfer devices such as pay on death bank accounts, transfer on death securities or even life policies with designated beneficiaries. In each case, you can nominate a beneficiary for the proceeds of the account/policy and the financial institution holding same will quickly arrange the transfer of the proceeds to the named beneficiary upon production of your death certificate. These methods provide a great source of readily available funds following your death.

Secondly, you could transfer your assets to a living trust. Assets held in a living trust will not become part of your probatable estate because the assets are not held in your name. This allows them to be quickly distributed to the beneficiaries of the trust following your death.

Thirdly, you can convert assets that you own solely into jointly owned assets. Where assets are jointly owned, it is possible to designate that a right of survivorship will apply to these assets. This means that when one of the joint owners die, the asset will pass directly to the surviving joint owner – without the need for probate. Of course, the joint owner can be a friend or relative; and the assets can comprise of anything from real estate to cash in a bank account.

Thus, in the same way as the other devices mentioned above, the surviving joint owner can quickly claim ownership of the asset following your death by simply producing a certified copy of your death certificate.

Resource

For further information on avoiding probate, see our book entitled "Make Your Own Living Trust & Avoid Probate". See page 198.

Planning for Incapacity – Power of Attorney for Finance and Property

A power of attorney is a legal document by which you appoint and authorize another person (usually a trusted friend, family member, colleague or adviser) to act on your behalf in the event that you become incapacitated.

In order for a power of attorney to apply when you are incapacitated, it will need to be stated to be a durable power of attorney. Ordinary powers of attorney cease to have legal effect once you become incapacitated. A durable power of attorney remains valid or, in some cases, only commences if you become incapacitated.

Durable powers of attorney come in two forms – a durable general power of attorney and a durable limited power of attorney. Under a durable general power of attorney, you can appoint an agent to whom you give authority to collect and disburse money on your behalf; operate your bank accounts; buy and sell property in your name; refurbish and rent out your property; and generally sign documents and deeds as your *alter ego*. It permits your agent to act as your authorized legal representative in relation to the whole cross-section of your legal and financial affairs, until such time as the authorization granted under the power of attorney is revoked or comes to an end.

You can of course limit the scope of your agent's authority by creating a durable limited power of attorney. This is similar to a durable general power of attorney except that, under the terms of this document, you can expressly limit the agent's authority to carrying out certain functions such as, for example, the management of your business, selling a property or another specific task.

Most responsible individuals plan how their property will be divided amongst their loved ones following their death. However, all of these plans can seem like a waste of time and effort if the individual, through an accident or illness, finds themselves in a position where they cannot manage their own affairs while they are still alive. The individual's inability to manage his or her own assets, in particular, could result in a substantial depletion of the value of those assets. This could, in turn, render meaningless the individual's plans for the distribution of his or her assets on death.

The individual's family could be left facing serious financial hardship due to their inability to access the individual's assets while he or she is still alive. What if the individual's signature is required to access the family savings? What if assets need to be sold to pay for his or her medical care…but because he or she cannot sign the relevant documents, the family cannot raise the funds.

You can avoid this situation entirely by simply granting a durable power of attorney to a close friend or family member. If the need arises, they can take charge of your affairs and ensure that they are managed in much the same way as you would have done in the circumstances.

Resource

For further information on powers of attorney, see our book entitled "Make Your Own Medical & Financial Powers of Attorney". See page 199.

Planning for Incapacity – Advance Healthcare Directives

Advance healthcares directives are used to instruct others regarding the medical care that you would like to receive should you find yourself in a position where you cannot communicate your own wishes regarding same.

There are two specific types of healthcare directive that should be considered as part of your estate plan, each with differing features. These are living wills and healthcare powers of attorney.

Living Wills

A living will is a legal document by which you can instruct healthcare providers with regard to your wishes about the use or non-use of certain life-prolonging medical procedures, in the event that you become terminally ill or permanently unconscious and unable to communicate your wishes.

For many, the purpose of a living will is to document their wish that life-sustaining treatment, including artificially or technologically supplied nutrition and hydration, be withheld or withdrawn if they are unable to make medical decisions on their own behalf and are suffering from a terminal illness or are in a permanent state of unconsciousness from which they are unlikely to recover.

The manner in which a living will works is quite straightforward. In most states, two doctors must personally examine you and agree that medical procedures will only prolong the dying process. If both doctors agree that this is the case, then certain medical procedures may be withdrawn or withheld, depending on the contents of your living will. Of course, the withdrawal of these procedures will result in death. However, it should be noted that living wills can also be used to instruct attending physicians to use all possible means and treatments to keep you alive.

Other names sometimes found for living wills include 'instructions', 'directive to physicians', 'declaration' and 'advance medical directive'.

Resource

For further information on living wills, see our book entitled "Make Your Own Living Will". See page 198.

Healthcare Powers of Attorney

One of the principal limitations of living wills is that they come into play only when you are either terminally ill or permanently unconscious and can't specifically tell your doctors what you want done. Moreover, they also only deal with the receipt or non-receipt of life sustaining treatments. They would not, for example, apply where you were temporarily unconscious due to a relatively minor accident.

Whereas with a healthcare power of attorney, you can appoint a person you know and trust to make and communicate decisions on the receipt or non-receipt of all forms of medical treatment on your behalf. You don't even have to be terminally ill or permanently unconscious. You simply need to be unable to communicate your healthcare preferences. When this occurs, your appointed agent is entitled to step up and make medical decisions on your behalf.

This authority is effective only when your attending physician determines that you have lost the capacity to make informed healthcare decisions for yourself. As long as you still have this capacity, you retain the right to make all medical and other healthcare decisions on your behalf.

In your healthcare power of attorney, you may also limit the healthcare decisions that your agent will have authority to make. The authority of your agent to make healthcare decisions for you will generally include the authority to give informed consent; refuse to give informed consent; or to withdraw informed consent for any care, treatment, service or procedure designed to maintain, diagnose, or treat a physical or mental condition.

 Resource

For further information on healthcare powers of attorney, see our kit entitled "Healthcare Power of Attorney & Living Kit". See www.enodare. com.

Reducing Taxes On Your Estate

A good estate plan will be structured in the most tax efficient manner to ensure that your estate pays as little in estate taxes as possible. Every amount paid in taxes is ultimately deducted from the amount payable from your estate to your loved ones. As such, it's very important, particularly where you have a valuable estate, that you seek tax advice when preparing your estate plan and that you utilize as many of the available tax planning opportunities as possible.

Conclusion

As you may have gathered, there are numerous benefits and satisfactions that can be derived from a good estate plan including:

- the provision of care and welfare of your immediate family;

- the transfer of property to your beneficiaries as quickly and inexpensively as possible;

- the reduction of taxes on your estate, and the resulting increase in the value of the gifts you make to your beneficiaries;

- the ability to choose the right executors and trustees for your estate;

- the minimizing of strain and uncertainty for your family;

- the pleasure of helping a favorite cause;

- the ability to manage the inheritances of family members/friends who need help and guidance with the management of their own affairs; and

- the avoidance of probate on your estate altogether!

In estate planning, money is not the root of all evil; it is procrastination that presents the real danger. If you procrastinate for too long and put off planning your estate, it becomes very unlikely that your property will be distributed entirely as you would have wished. However, it also becomes very likely that your family and friends will suffer personally and financially. So don't procrastinate – take some simple steps to begin the process of creating your estate plan!

APPENDIX 1:
FUNERAL PLANNING CHECKLIST

CD-ROM & Downloadable Forms

Blank copies of all of the forms contained in this book are available on the CD-ROM which accompanies this book. Alternatively all forms can be downloaded from the enodare website.

Web: http://www.enodare.com/downloadarea/

Unlock Code: FUR49712

enodare

APPENDIX 1

FUNERAL PLANNING CHECKLIST

Funeral Planning Checklist - The Basics

Planning a funeral is a difficult and complicated process which is made even more difficult by the emotional stress that accompanies the death of a loved one. Fortunately, many of the arrangements can be made ahead of time, thereby decreasing the burden on those left behind. Use the checklist below when discussing funeral plans with your loved ones to make sure that your final wishes are carried out.

Pre-planning – Funeral

- Assemble personal information for an obituary

- Ensure you have prepared a last will and testament

- Choose a charity for donations

- Choose a funeral home

- Decide on burial or cremation

- Select a casket or cremation container

- Select a burial vault or cremation urn

- Decide on the location of service

- Decide on the type of service

- Decide on family viewing of public viewing

- Decide on clothing

- Decide on music, hymns and prayers to be read. You may also like to decide on who is to do the selected readings

- Select a memorial register

- Transportation should be considered such as a funeral coach, transport for family and loved ones, the clergy car, pallbearers etc.

- Decide on a cemetery

- Choose a burial or cremation plot

- Select a memorial or grave marker and inscription

- Arrange the post funeral reception

Pre-planning Frequently Asked Questions

Can I pre-pay for a funeral?

Yes, most funeral homes allow pre-payment and pre-planning. Funeral homes have different funding options that will help minimize the financial strain your family and loved ones will experience when confronted with funeral expenses. Generally funeral homes will create a funeral trust to cover payment of the funeral when the time arrives.

How does the pre-payment process work?

You pay for the selected products and services in advance or by installments depending on your arrangements with the funeral home. The monies are held in a trust in your name. These funds are often invested or placed in a high interest account in order to keep pace with inflation. You may cancel the trust at anytime and receive a full refund including any interest earned. This, however, should be verified with your funeral home.

What if I move to another state?

You can change the terms of your trust to make payment to a different funeral home if you move. It's very straightforward. In most cases, the trusts used are government ones and the funeral homes are merely acting as agents which makes the trusts completely transferable.

What other documents should I keep on hand?

A last will and testament - As part of any final arrangement, it is vital that you prepare a last will and testament. Preparing a last will and testament will allow you to properly plan for the disposition of your assets and, in many cases, provide basic details for your funeral service.

If you die without making a valid last will and testament, you will lose control over who your assets are given to, who will mind your children and your estate will be substantially depleted due to the high costs of intestate administration. Making a valid will is the only way for you to provide for the special needs of your family and save your estate thousands of dollars in unnecessary intestate administration expenses.

It is important to remember that your will may not be read until after your burial so ensure that your funeral wishes are made known in advance and that your funeral plan is available to those who will be organizing your funeral.

While funeral costs increase annually, people still fail to plan for the inevitable. Why is this?

There are several reasons for this:

- Many people do not preplan their funeral simply because they are unaware of the options available to them. A visit to the local funeral home would give them a clear picture of funeral requirements and costs and more importantly details of payment options such as installments, trusts and insurance.

- People do not know where to go for advice and guidance.

- People refuse to accept the inevitability of death and therefore procrastinate in making funeral arrangements. This however means that funeral arrangements will have to be made by someone who is already grieving – someone who understandably may not make the best choices for you.

- The substantial cost of funerals often deters people from making funeral arrangements.

- Some people would prefer if their funeral was arranged by family members and then paid for from their estate.

APPENDIX 2:
FUNERAL ARRANGEMENT FORM

APPENDIX 2

FUNERAL ARRANGEMENT FORM

OF

_____

PERSONAL DETAILS

FULL NAME (FIRST, MIDDLE, LAST)

Name _____

ADDRESS

Street _____

_____

City _____

State _____

Zip _____

NEXT OF KIN OR CONTACT PERSON

NAME

Name _____

Relationship _____

ADDRESS

Street _____

_____

City _____

State _____

Zip   _____

Phone No.   _____

LAST WILL & TESTAMENT

(Initial one choice only)

_____   I have written a Will. It can be located at _____
_____. To the extent that there are any funeral arrangement instructions in my Will, please treat this document as expanding on those wishes, with the instructions in my Will taking precedent.

_____   I have not written a Will.

FUNERAL DETAILS

(1)   Is it your wish to die at home?
YES _____ / NO _____ (Initial one choice only)

If yes, do you want to have your body retained at home until the funeral if possible?
YES _____ / NO _____ (Initial one choice only)

If yes, specify any special requests here: _____
_____
_____
_____
_____

If no, would you like to have your body on display in a funeral home? YES

_____ / NO _____ (Initial one choice only)

If yes, would you like to have an open casket (circumstances permitting) or a closed casket?

Initial one choice: _____ I would prefer an open casket.

_____ I would prefer a closed casket.

(2)   If you die in a hospital or nursing home, do you want your body to be returned home prior to the funeral? YES _____ / NO _____ (Initial one choice only)

If so please indicate how long for :

_____

(3)   In most situations, nursing staff lay out the body. Where it is possible, would you prefer someone else to do this, or perhaps assist? YES _____ / NO _____ (Initial one choice only)

If yes, the please give the following information regarding the person that you want to assist with the lay out of your body:-

Name: _____

Address: _____

_____

_____

_____

Telephone No: _____

(4)   Do you wish your body to be embalmed? YES _____ / NO _____ (Initial one choice only)

(Note: If you choose woodland burial, embalming may not be accepted. Embalming is often referred to as 'cosmetic' or 'hygienic' treatment by funeral personnel).

(5)   Have you already purchased a casket? YES _____ / NO _____ (Initial one choice only)

If yes, it can be located by contacting:

Name: _____

Address: _____

_____

_____

_____

Telephone No: _____

If no, do you have any preferences as to the type of casket you require? YES _____ / NO _____ (Initial one choice only)

If yes, please insert details of the type of casket you would prefer. You should make reference to the materials used (ash, pine, bronze), color and style you would like _____

_____

_____

_____

_____

_____

(Standard coffins are made of veneered chipboard, although cardboard, pure wood and wicker are available, as well as a wool shroud (burial only) – it is advisable to check details, prices and availability before you decide.)

(Other alternatives that are more personal are available such as if you require an unusual or artist painted coffin then details of the supplier and design must be arranged in advance – and details added to this plan. Alternatively you can make your own, if you prefer).

(6)   For your funeral, how would you like to have your body transported?

(Initial one of (a) to (c) or complete section (d))

(a) By hearse   YES _____

(b) By horse drawn hearse   YES _____

(c) By motorcycle hearse   YES _____

(d) Other, please specify_____.

(7)   Do you want a limousine or the funeral service provider's cars to be used for the transportation of your immediate family during the funeral service? YES _____ / NO _____ (Initial one choice only)

(8)   Would you prefer family members and close friends to act as pall bearers for your casket? YES _____ / NO _____ (Initial one choice only)

If yes, specify the names of the people that you would prefer (in order of preference) to act as pall bearers (four to six people will be needed) at your funeral: _____

_____

_____

_____

If no, would you prefer to use pall bearers provided by the funeral director?
YES _____ / NO _____ (Initial one choice only)

(9)   Do you want to leave wreath and flower choice to mourners?
YES _____ / NO _____ (Initial one choice only)

Do you want family flowers only?
YES _____ / NO _____ (Initial one choice only)

Do you want no flowers?
YES _____ / NO _____ (Initial one choice only)

If you choose to have no flowers or family flowers only, would you like other mourners to make donations to a favorite charity in lieu of flowers?
YES _____ / NO _____ (Initial one choice only)

If yes, please insert of the charities (in order of preference) that you would like to have donations made to: _____

_____

_____

_____

(10)   Do you want your death and funeral announced in any specific publications?
YES _____ / NO _____ (Initial one choice only)

If yes, which publications would you like the announcement made in and how many entries would you like made? _____

_____

_____

_____

_____

(11)   Do you have any other special requests?

YES _____ / NO _____ (Initial one choice only)

If yes, please give details _____

_____

_____

_____

_____

THE FUNERAL SERVICE

(1)   Do you require a funeral service?

YES _____ / NO _____ (Initial one choice only)

If yes, before going to the crematorium or place of burial, do you want a service in church or chapel first?

If yes, give details of the service you want: _____

_____

_____

_____

_____

(There may be additional church fees, organist fees, etc. to pay. If a Church /Chapel service is held first, a short committal ceremony will normally occur at the Crematorium or place of burial, which takes about five minutes).

(2)   What religion / spiritual belief / philosophy should the service be based upon?_____

_____

(3)   Do you have a minister or other person in mind to officiate at the service? This can be a friend or relative, if desired. If yes, insert details: _____

_____

_____

_____

_____

(4)   If you wish to guide those arranging the service, enter the following details:-

Attendees: Is the service open to all? YES _____ / NO _____ (Initial one choice only)

If no, insert details of any desired restrictions: _____

_____

_____

_____

_____

Music: Do you want any specific music or hymns played at the service? YES _____ / NO _____ (Initial one choice only)

If yes, insert details of any desired music: _____

_____

_____

_____

_____

Readings: Do you want any specific readings (scriptures, poems, etc) READ at your service? YES _____ / NO _____ (Initial one choice only)

If yes, insert details of any desired readings: _____

_____

_____

_____

_____

General: If you have any other requirements, insert same here:

_____

_____

_____

(5)   Do you want a speech or eulogy about your life read at the service? YES _____ / NO _____ (Initial one choice only)

If yes, the text should be attached to the back of this plan, or the name of who will compose(the address) should be entered here: _____

_____

_____

_____

_____

(6)   Is there any particular person(s) you wish to be invited to the service, who

could otherwise be omitted? YES _____ / NO _____ (Initial one choice only)

If yes, insert the names and contact details of any such person(s) _____

_____

_____

_____

_____

(7)   Are there any specific rituals or features that you want included in the service (Items placed on coffin, photograph displayed in the church etc.)? YES _____ / NO _____ (Initial one choice only)

If yes, insert details of any such rituals or features: _____

_____

_____

_____

_____

FINAL DISPOSITION

(1)   Would you prefer to have your remains buried or cremated?

Initial one choice only: _____ I would prefer to have my remains buried. If you choose to have your remains buried, complete the section below entitled "Burial".

OR

_____ I would prefer to have my remains cremated. If you choose to have your remains cremate, complete the section below entitled "Cremation".

BURIAL

(1)   Enter details of your preferred place of burial:

_____

_____

_____

_____

(2)   Have you already purchased a plot in this cemetery? YES _____ / NO _____
(Initial one choice only)

If yes, insert the following details:
Location of plot::_____

_____

Type of plot:_____

_____

Location of deds:_____

_____

(3)   Is the grave a new grave? YES _____ / NO _____ (Initial   one
choice only)

If no, insert details of the person already buried in this grave and the date on
which they were buried: _____

_____

_____

_____

_____

(4)   Have you purchased a grave liner or burial vault? YES _____ / NO
_____ (Initial   one choice only)

If yes, it can be located by contacting:

Name: _____

Address: _____

_____

_____

_____

Telephone No: _____

(5)   Have you purchaseD a headstone or marker? YES _____ / NO _____ (Initial one choice only)

If yes, it can be located by contacting:

Name: _____

Address: _____

_____

_____

_____

Telephone No: _____

If no, do you have a specific memorial in mind? YES _____ / NO _____ (Initial one choice only)

If yes, insert details: _____

_____

_____

_____

_____

Have you checked the cemetery's rules and regulations to see if this type of headstone or marker is permitted? YES _____ / NO _____ (Initial one choice only)

If yes, are you sure this is permitted on the above grave? YES _____ / NO _____ (Initial one choice only)

Insert the contact details of any mason you have identified to supply and fit the memorial:

Name: _____

Address: _____

_____

_____

_____

Telephone No: _____

CREMATION

(1) After cremation, what would you like to have done with your remains? Insert details here: _____

_____

_____

_____

_____

(2)   If an urn or casket is required, do you require a specific type? Insert
         details here: _____

         _____

         _____

         _____

         _____

SUBSEQUENT MEMORIAL SERVICE

(1)   Would you like a memorial service, or some sort of gathering, to be held after
         your death? YES _____ / NO _____ (Initial   one choice only)

         If yes, please provide details: _____

         _____

         _____

         _____

         _____

         (Enclose details on separate sheet if you wish).

COMMEMORATION

(1)   Do you require a form of commemoration after your death? YES _____ / NO
         _____ (Initial   one choice only)

         If yes, please provide details: _____

         _____

         _____

         _____

         _____

         (This may include a grave memorial, book of remembrance, etc. or may extend
         to a donation, endowment, gift to parish or church, or the planting of a tree.

If the information is given in a will or is confidential, there is no need to give details).

LAST WISHES

(1)   Is there any last wish, or words which have remained unsaid, that you would like to say now? YES _____ / NO _____ (Initial one choice only)

If yes, please specify: _____

_____

_____

_____

_____

(2)   Have you left any final letters? YES _____ / NO _____ (Initial one choice only)

If yes, state the location of these letters and to whom they are addressed? _____

_____

_____

_____

_____

PAYMENT OF FUNERAL COSTS

(1)   Have you set up any means by which the cost of your funeral can be discharged? YES _____ / NO _____ (Initial one choice only)

If yes, please provide precise details (including account numbers): _____

_____

_____

_____

_____

ADDITIONAL INSTRUCTIONS

(1)   Please add any additional instructions here: _____

_____

_____

_____

_____

_____

_____

_____

_____

_____

SUPPORTING DOCUMENTATION

If you have any supporting documentation such as receipts, plot title deeds, readings, music pieces etc that you wish to attach to this funeral plan please do so. Otherwise the exact location of all relevant documents should be listed.

APPENDIX 3:
FUNERAL COST PLANNER

CD-ROM & Downloadable Forms

Blank copies of all of the forms contained in this book are available on the CD-ROM which accompanies this book. Alternatively all forms can be downloaded from the enodare website.

Web: http://www.enodare.com/downloadarea/

Unlock Code: FUR49712

enodare

APPENDIX 3

FUNERAL COST PLANNER

Funeral Home "A"   Cost $

Removal: _____

Facility use: _____

Arrangement conference: _____

Documentation & registration: _____

Body preparation: _____

Additional extras:

_____: _____

_____: _____

_____: _____

_____: _____

_____: _____

Cremation cost: _____

Container: _____

Total cost: _____

Additional notes: _____

_____

_____

_____

_____

_____

Funeral Home "B"   Cost $

Removal: _____

Facility use: _____

Arrangement conference: _____

Documentation & registration: _____

Body preparation: _____

Additional extras:

_____: _____

_____: _____

_____: _____

_____: _____

_____: _____

Cremation cost: _____

Container: _____

Total cost: _____

Additional notes: _____

_____

_____

_____

_____

_____

Funeral Home "C"   Cost $

Removal: _____

Facility use: _____

Arrangement conference: _____

Documentation & registration: _____

Body preparation: _____

Additional extras:

_____: _____

_____: _____

_____: _____

_____: _____

_____: _____

Cremation cost: _____

Container: _____

Total cost: _____

Additional Notes: _____

_____

_____

_____

_____

_____

Funeral Home "D"   Cost $

Removal: _____

Facility use: _____

Arrangement conference: _____

Documentation & registration: _____

Body preparation: _____

Additional extras:

_____: _____

_____: _____

_____: _____

_____: _____

_____: _____

Cremation cost: _____

Container: _____

Total cost: _____

Additional notes: _____

_____

_____

_____

_____

_____

APPENDIX 4:
INFORMATION REQUIRED FOR REGISTRATION OF A DEATH

CD-ROM & Downloadable Forms

Blank copies of all of the forms contained in this book are available on the CD-ROM which accompanies this book. Alternatively all forms can be downloaded from the enodare website.

Web: http://www.enodare.com/downloadarea/

Unlock Code: FUR49712

enodare

Appendix 4

APPENDIX 4

INFORMATION REQUIRED FOR REGISTRATION OF A DEATH

In the United States, authorities with responsibility for the registration of births, deaths, marriages, divorces, fetal deaths, and induced terminations of pregnancy (abortions) reside in each state (as well as in cities such as New York City and Washington, D.C.) and in Puerto Rico, the U.S. Virgin Islands, Guam, American Samoa, and the Commonwealth of the Northern Marianas.

Each of these states and municipals are the full legal proprietors of the vital statistics records and the information contained therein, and are responsible for maintaining registries according to state law, and issuing copies of birth, marriage, divorce, and death certificates.

When a death occurs, a physician or coroner attending the death must complete a medical certificate of death and then hand it over to the funeral director or person organizing the funeral.

To register a death a family member must complete the information required to register a death and then pass the information to the state office responsible for registration of deaths. This information is usually submitted along with the medical certificate of death. Once the death is registered, the next of kin or an executor of estate may apply for a death certificate to be issued to them.

APPENDIX 5:

MISCELLANEOUS PERSONAL DETAILS AND CONTACT LIST

CD-ROM & Downloadable Forms

Blank copies of all of the forms contained in this book are available on the CD-ROM which accompanies this book. Alternatively all forms can be downloaded from the enodare website.

Web: http://www.enodare.com/downloadarea/

Unlock Code: FUR49712

enodare

Appendix 5

APPENDIX 5

MISCELLANEOUS PERSONAL DETAILS AND CONTACT LIST

Personal Details

Full Name: _____

Address: _____

City: State/Province: Zip/Postal Code: _____

Home Phone Number: _____

Birth Date (month, day, year): _____

Birthplace (city, state/province): _____

Social Security/Social Insurance Number: _____

Marital Status (single, married, widowed, divorced): _____

Spouse's Full Name: _____

Social Security/Social Insurance Number: _____

Spouse's Birth Date (month, day, year): _____

Marriage Date and Location: _____

Father's Full Name: _____

Father's Birth Date (month, day, year): _____

Mother's Full Name: _____

Mother's Birth Date (month, day, year): _____

Extended Family

Children (list oldest to youngest, include spouses and resident city): _____
_____

Number of Grandchildren & Names: _____
_____

Number of Great Grandchildren & Names: _____
_____

Number of Great-Great-Grandchildren & Names: _____
_____

Brothers/sisters (list oldest to youngest, include spouses and resident city): _____
_____
_____
_____
_____
_____

Other Contacts

Family Physician: _____

Physician's Address: _____

Physician's Phone Number: _____

Next of Kin or Executor: _____

Relationship to Deceased: _____

Address: Phone Number: _____

Additional Instructions: _____

Work History

Current or Last Occupation: _____

Current or Last Employer: _____

Years Employed: _____

Date of Retirement:_____

Military Service

Branch of Service: _____

War: _____

Discharge Papers Filed at: _____

Rank: Served or Stationed at: _____

Eligible for Veteran's Disability (yes or no): _____

Religious Affiliation/Memberships

Religious Affiliations: _____

Church Groups/Membership: _____

Clubs/Lodge Memberships: _____

Professional Organizations: _____

Unions or Civic Group: _____

Other: _____

Funeral Information

Contact Person: _____

Address: _____

Phone: _____

Type of Service Selected: _____

Contemporary Service: _____

Place of Service (funeral home, church, name of church): _____
_____

Memorial Service (funeral home/church): _____
_____

No Service: _____

Type of Disposition (burial, entombment, cremation, or body donation): _____
_____

Name & Location of Cemetery/Mausoleum: _____
_____

Description of Lot or Mausoleum: _____

Additional information required (newspaper obituary placement, music, and
special readings): _____
_____
_____

When your death occurs you may wish to inform important people in your life as
soon as possible. By completing the form below as part of your funeral planning
arrangements, you will ensure that those arranging your funeral will know
directly who you wish to inform about your death.

Immediate Contacts at Time of Death

Executor: _____

Name: Telephone Number: E-Mail: _____

Employer: _____

Relations: _____

Friends: _____

Within Seven Days

Attorney/Lawyer: _____

Life Insurance Agents: _____

Other: _____

INDEX

Other Great Books from Enodare's Estate Planning Series

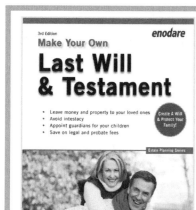

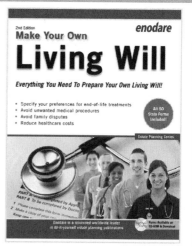

Make Your Own Last Will & Testament

Make Your Own Living Trust & Avoid Probate

Make Your Own Living Will

By making a will, you can provide for the distribution of your assets to your love ones, appoint guardians to care for your children, provide for the management of gifts to young adults and children, specify how your debts are to be paid following your death, make funeral arrangements and much more.

This book will guide you through the entire process of making a will. It contains all the forms that you will need to make a valid legal will, simply and easily.

Living trusts are used to distribute a person's assets after they die in a manner that avoids the costs, delays and publicity of probate. They also cater for the management of property during periods of incapacity.

This book will guide you step-by-step through the process of creating your very own living trust, transferring assets to your living trust and subsequently managing those assets.

All relevant forms are included.

Do you want a say in what life sustaining medical treatments you receive during periods in which you are incapacitated and either in a permanent state of unconsciousness or suffering from a terminal illness? Well if so, you must have a living will!

This book will introduce you to living wills, the types of medical procedures that they cover, the matters that you need to consider when making them and, of course, provide you with all the relevant forms you need to make your own living will!

Other Great Books from Enodare's Estate Planning Series

Make Your Own Medical & Financial Powers of Attorney

The importance of having powers of attorney is often underappreciated. They allow people you trust to manage your property and financial affairs during periods in which you are incapacitated; as well as make medical decisions on your behalf based on the instructions in your power of attorney document. This ensures that your affairs don't go unmanaged and you don't receive any unwanted medical treatments.

This book provides all the necessary documents and step-by-step instructions to make a power of attorney to cover virtually any situation!

How to Probate an Estate - A Step-By-Step Guide for Executors

This book is essential reading for anyone contemplating acting as an executor of someone's estate!

Learn about the various stages of probate and what an executor needs to do at each stage to successfully navigate his way through to closing the estate and distributing the deceased's assets.

You will learn how an executor initiates probate, locates and manages assets, deals with debt and taxes, distributes assets, and much more. This is a fantastic step-by-step guide through the entire process!

Estate Planning Essentials

This book is a must read for anyone who doesn't already have a comprehensive estate plan.

It will show you the importance of having wills, trusts, powers of attorney and living wills in your estate plan. You will learn about the probate process, why people are so keen to avoid it and lots of simple methods you can actually use to do so. You will learn about reducing estate taxes and how best to provide for young beneficiaries and children.

This book is a great way to get you started on the way to making your own estate plan.

Will Writer - Estate Planning Software

Everything You Need to Create Your Estate Plan

Product Description

Enodare's Estate Planning Software helps you create wills, living trusts, living wills, powers of attorney and more from the comfort of your own home and without the staggering legal fees!

Through the use of a simple question and answer process, we'll guide you step-by-step through the process of preparing your chosen document. It only takes a few minutes of your time and comprehensive help and information is available at every stage of the process.

Product Features:

 Last Wills

Make gifts to your family, friends and charities, make funeral arrangements, appoint executors, appoint guardians to care for your minor children, make property management arrangements for young beneficiaries, release people from debts, and much more.

 Living Trusts

Make gifts to your family and friends, make property management arrangements for young beneficiaries, transfer assets tax efficiently with AB Trusts, and much more.

 Living Wills

Instruct doctors as to your choices regarding the receipt or non-receipt of medical treatments designed to prolong your life.

www.enodare.com

✓ Healthcare Power of Attorney

Appoint someone you trust to make medical decisions for you if you become mentally incapacitated.

Ensure Your Family's Protected

✓ Power of Attorney for Finance and Property

Appoint someone you trust to manage your financial affairs if you become mentally incapacitated, or if you are unable to do so for any reason.

✓ And More.........

Enodare's Will Writer software also includes documents such as self proving Affidavits, Deeds of Assignment, Certifications of Trust, Estate Planning Worksheet, Revocation forms and more.

The documents are valid in all states except Louisiana.

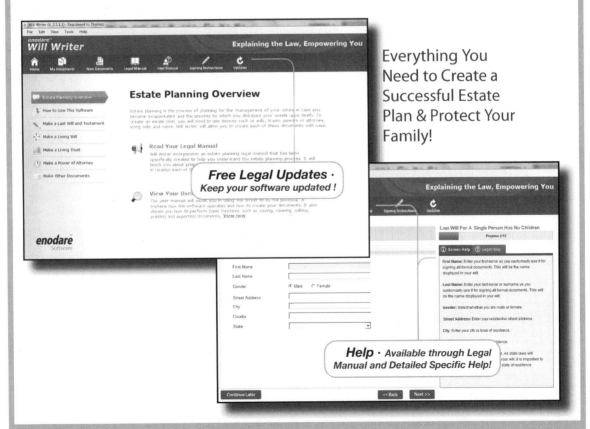

Everything You Need to Create a Successful Estate Plan & Protect Your Family!

Entrepreneur's Guide to Starting a Business

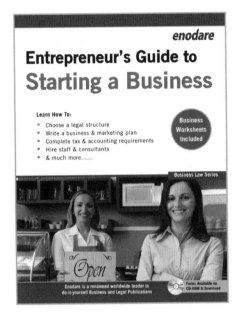

Entrepreneur's Guide to Starting a Business takes the fear of the unknown out of starting your new business and provides a treasure chest of information that will help you be successful from the very start.

First-time entrepreneurs face a daunting challenge in identifying all of the issues that must be addressed and mastered when starting a new business. If any item slips through the cracks, or is handled improperly, it could bring a new company crashing to the ground. Entrepreneur's Guide to Starting a Business helps you meet that challenge by walking you through all of the important aspects of successfully launching your own business.

When you finish reading this book, not alone will you know the step-by-step process needed to turn your business idea and vision into a successful reality, but you'll also have a wealth of practical knowledge about corporate structures, business & marketing plans, e-commerce, hiring staff & external advisors, finding commercial property, sales & marketing, legal & financial matters, tax and much more.

- Comprehensive overview of all major aspects of starting a new business

- Covers every stage of the process, from writing your business plan to marketing and selling your new product

- Plain English descriptions of complex subject matters

- Real-world case study showing you how things play out in an actual new business environment

enodare

NEW TITLE

Personal Budget Kit

Budgeting Made Easy

In this kit, we'll guide you step-by-step through the process of creating and living with a personal budget. We'll show you how analyze how you receive and spend your money and to set goals, both short and long-term.

You'll learn how to gain control of your personal cash flow. You'll discover when you need to make adjustments to your budget and how to do it wisely. Most of all, this kit will show you that budgeting isn't simply about adding limitations to your living but rather the foundation for living better by maximizing the resources you have.

This Personal Budget Kit provides you with step-by-step instructions, detailed information and all the budget worksheets and spreadsheets necessary to identify and understand your spending habits, reduce your expenses, set goals, prepare personal budgets, monitor your progress and take control over your finances.

- Reduce your spending painlessly and effortlessly

- Pay off your debts early

- Improve your credit rating

- Save & invest money

- Set & achieve financial goals

- Eliminate financial worries

Budget Planning Spreadsheets Included

enodare

•NEW TITLE

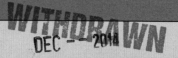